A CERTAIN

A CERTAIN RUMOUR

Learning to Live Hopefully
Ever After

Russell Rook

Authentic

MILTON KEYNES ● COLORADO SPRINGS
● HYDERABAD

Equipping the Church for action

Copyright © 2008 Russell Rook

14 13 12 11 10 09 08   7 6 5 4 3 2 1

First published 2008 by Spring Harvest Publishing Division and
Authentic Media
9 Holdom Avenue, Bletchley, Milton Keynes, MK1 1QR, UK
1820 Jet Stream Drive, Colorado Springs, CPO 80921, USAOM
Authentic Media, Medchal Road, Jeedimetla Village,
Secunderabad 500 055, A.P., India
www.authenticmedia.co.uk
Authentic Media is a division of IBS-STL U.K., limited by
guarantee, with its Registered Office at Kingstown Broadway,
Carlisle, Cumbria CA3 0HA. Registered in England & Wales No.
1216232. Registered charity 270162

The right of Russell Rook to be identified as the Author of this work has
been asserted by him in accordance with the Copyright,
Designs and Patents Act 1988

British Library Cataloguing in Publication Data
A catalogue record for this book is available from the
British Library
ISBN: 978-1-85078-779-2

Unless otherwise stated, Scripture quotations are taken from the
HOLY BIBLE, NEW INTERNATIONAL VERSION. Copyright © 1973,
1978, 1984 by International Bible Society. Used by permission of Hodder
& Stoughton Publishers, a division of Hodder Headline Ltd. All rights
reserved. 'NIV' is a registered trademark of International Bible Society. UK
trademark number 1448790

Cover Design by David Lund
Print Management by Adare
Printed in Great Britain by J.H. Haynes & Co., Sparkford

To Nicola Garnham
It has been an inspiration to watch you walk with Jesus in these past months. Thank you for teaching me what it means to live hopefully ever after.

Contents

Acknowledgements   ix

I'll Get My Coat   xi

1. Hope Hits the Road   1
2. Hope After Death   26
3. Hope Before Life   52
4. Hope in the Desert   77
5. Hope Comes to Dinner   98
6. Hope in the Future   122

Acknowledgements

As always, the list of people that need thanking is almost as long as the book itself.

I first must express much gratitude to all those who helped to put this project on the road. To Sherri Golisky, for many vital contributions, constant support and feedback – thanks for your hard work, patience and flexibility. To Matt Little, for the many road trips, helpful research and preparation of the final manuscript. For the ever-encouraging and always-inspirational Stephen Holmes, as you once said to me, 'There are some students you never get rid of.' To Richard Bauckham, Pete Broadbent, Steve Chalke, Ian Coffey, Chuck Day, Ruth Dearnley, Sarah Doyle, Philip Garnham, Alan Johnson, Mark Knight, Adam Knuckey, Jeff Lucas, Rachael Orrell and everyone else who has helped to direct and sustain these exacting eschatological expeditions. To Mark Finnie, Charlotte Hubback, Kath Williams and the whole Authentic team, thanks for getting this book on and off the shelf.

Big thanks go to Louise Macdonald and Meghan Rapp for providing great life-support. To the ALOVE UK team for being the best bunch anyone could wish to work with; to all my colleagues at The Salvation Army, for your support and guidance; and to the Spring Harvest Head Office team, for your friendship, encouragement and patience. Thanks to everyone for everything at Raynes Park Community Church.

Last and by no means least, to my family and friends: thanks for putting up with the long silences, frequent mood swings and the unfeasibly busy diary which has accompanied this project. To Ma, thanks for the use of your office and laptop. To Charlotte, Joe and Toby, you are a constant source of joy; thank you for helping me to live so happily and hopefully.

I'll Get My Coat

I can't work out whether it's one of my strengths or weaknesses. If you ask me, I think I'm pretty good at it – leaving the house, that is. I'm certainly fast. I confess that my speed is often generated by the fact that I'm running ten minutes late – either that or by my general impatience and dislike of stillness. My wife and kids, on the other hand, would probably tell you that I am very bad at it. They'd say I get grumpy, impatient and shout too much. They'd no doubt back this up by citing the numerous times I've forgotten something and have had to return home to pick it up, thus further delaying our arrival. 'More haste less speed', they say. All I want to know is why it takes so long to put on a coat, find a handbag and turn off the lights!

As with those exceedingly long journeys from the house to the car, I've never enjoyed long book introductions. Halfway through the first paragraph I'm usually shouting, 'Can we please get this show on the road?' This can cause my fellow commuters to look slightly nervous, but that's beside the point. For readers like me, I promise to try and keep this introduction short. After all, the sooner we get past this bit, the sooner we can hit the road. In the mean time, it makes some sense to let you know what you're in for.

Luke's gospel doesn't say why Cleopas and his companion left the house. Nor does he explain if they were in a rush. If certain scholars are correct in identifying his fellow traveller as his 'other half', then I suspect it may have taken an age to get going. However, such trivial speculation is not important right now. What is important is that a few hours and seven miles later, the lives of these individuals and the world at large had changed forever. In these chapters we will retrace this historic hike.

As with all road trips, the journey is only as good as the company you keep along the way. While I am sure that Cleopas and his companion were happy to share the walk together, the addition of another traveller transformed an unexceptional wander into a voyage of divine discovery. Later that day, when they discover the identity of their mystery journeymen, everything becomes clear. And I mean everything.

Having joined them along the road, Jesus proceeds to retell and teach the whole Old Testament story. Here, in one short walk to Emmaus, we have what must have been the most electrifying and fast-paced Bible study ever. How Jesus crams it in, we'll never know. The biblical scholar Tom Wright is famed for his description of the Bible as a meta-narrative about monotheism, elections and eschatology. Put simply, the Bible is God's story. This big fat story, or meta-narrative, uses three grand themes to help us understand life, the universe and everything. The first, monotheism, concerns the one true God who made the heavens and the earth. The second, election, concerns the one people through whom God chose to reveal himself to the world. And the third, eschatology, features the high hopes that God has for creation. While our journey will take in all three of these grand themes, it is the third that will concern us most. In this book we will retell God's story of hope for the world.

As we journey with Jesus and Cleopas down the road to Emmaus, we will stop to admire some of the defining events, important landmarks and dazzling scenery of the biblical story. In the short time we have available we will endeavour to survey the whole of God's story. Our main aim in this quick route march through the Bible is to discover God's hope. By rehearsing the Bible story, listening in to Cleopas' discussion and reflecting on our own journey we will look to become ever more hopeful followers of Christ.

We begin with the events of the crucifixion (Chapter 1). Early that day Cleopas and his companion had set out with heavy hearts. With Jesus dead, or so they thought, the world appeared a darker, less hopeful place. The first thing Jesus does when he draws alongside the travellers is to help them come to terms with the events of the past days. By listening in on these discussions we'll discover how the death of God's Son brings fresh hope to his world.

In the second stage of our journey (Chapter 2), we will address the rumours of Jesus' resurrection. Cleopas and co. wandered along, left to wonder where Christ had gone. Was he simply dead, would he rise or had he risen? Jesus chooses to explain why these things had to take place long before he reveals his identity. In this part of the journey we discover the key to all human hoping. From now on, death holds no sting for us because Jesus is alive.

Having shown how all human hopes are fulfilled in the story of the first Easter, Jesus takes his friends back to the dawn of time to demonstrate where God's hopes begin. In Chapter 3 we will travel to look at the hope that God has had for us and our world since the beginning of history.

Moving forward ever quickly, Jesus jumps from creation to exodus, from the garden of Eden to the Egypt of the Pharaohs. In Chapter 4, we'll explore the role that the exodus story plays in the lives of God's people. With Jesus' help we'll reflect on our own stories and think about how they can provide us with God's hope for the future.

Then, taking the single largest leap in our journey so far, we'll join Jesus, Cleopas and his companion as they a share a meal together in Emmaus. In Chapter 5 we'll consider what it means to become part of the church and, as such, to find ourselves written in to the story of Christ's resurrection. From now on we become God's story and the hope of the world.

Finally, no journey to hope would be complete without some talk of the future. In our final chapter we'll look at what happens next. We'll join Cleopas as he returns to Jerusalem to share his good news with the disciples and we'll follow his progress as he goes on to help lead the church in Jerusalem. Most important of all we'll record the eternal impact that he and his friends make as they realize God's hopes for the whole world and implement God's perfect plan. In these final moments we ourselves confront our single greatest challenge. Here we'll stop to ask how our lives and churches will help the world to live hopefully ever after.

A number of years ago, two friends of mine tried to adopt an African baby called Zodwa. Zodwa had been orphaned when her parents had died of AIDS. Having failed in their attempt to adopt the child, Phil and Wendy, being visionary types, decided that they would set up a charity to raise money for the twelve million children who have been orphaned by AIDS. They called the charity HOPE HIV, a truly perfect name. While it is impossible for any of us to comprehend the complexities of the AIDS pandemic in sub-Saharan Africa, one word can change the situation. Although Cleopas' walk to Emmaus was short in distance, the scope of his journey was immense. Under the power of hope he travelled from death to resurrection and from creation to perfection. I hope that, in retracing his steps, you too will catch such a view.

As you grab your coat and rush out the door to join Cleopas on the road, I would offer four simple prayers. I pray that you'll enjoy this short walk to hope. I pray that the journey will enable you to explore the hopeful news of Christ's resurrection and the hope-filled words of God's story. I pray that the discussions along the way will help you to discover God's hopes for your own life, church and community. Most of all, I pray that, in your walk with Jesus, you will discover the secret of living hopefully ever after.

1

Hope Hits the Road

The Road Ahead

In this chapter we will look at the events surrounding Christ's crucifixion. As we retrace Cleopas' travels from Jerusalem to Emmaus we'll see how God can transform the most ordinary journey into the most extraordinary of adventures. In just a few miles and a matter of hours, Jesus teaches a hopeless Cleopas to live hopefully ever after and changes the direction of history. Before delving deeper into the events of the day, however, we need to ask what led Cleopas to follow Jesus in the first place. What did he hope to find with Jesus?

As did the rest of Jesus' followers, Cleopas hoped that Jesus might direct him to God's kingdom. With Cleopas, then, we will explore the expectations of God's people as they prayed for his kingdom to come. For Cleopas and every other disciple, the road to eternal hopefulness begins with relinquishing human hopes for the infinitely bigger hope that God makes available in Christ.

> Now that same day two of them were going to a village called Emmaus, about seven miles from Jerusalem (Lk. 24:13).

Where are we going?

The journey to Emmaus began in Jerusalem. We know that the disciples were in Jerusalem reeling from the shockwaves of their leader's death. We don't know why Cleopas and his companion set out for Emmaus, but we know they returned to Jerusalem at once. A wasted trip? Hardly. For Cleopas and every Christian since, it is the journey itself that is remarkable. It is a life-changing stretch of road.

A few months ago I visited a friend. Greetings exchanged, John asked whether I would like a coffee. Without a second thought, we jumped in his car and sped off to the nearest branch of a well-known caffeine dealer. As we were driving the five miles back to his office, something dawned on me. Ten years ago, accepting the offer of a cup of coffee entailed nothing more than a trip to the kitchen. But now we often reject this quick, simple and cost-effective route in favour of an altogether longer journey. Back then, spending time in traffic, money on fuel and £3.00 on a tall, skinny, mocha-whoppa-frappa-whappacino with extra whipped cream and chocolate flake would have been tantamount to insanity, no matter how tantalizing the beverage or its title. But here and now, it all seems completely normal.

Now if John had suggested walking to that coffee shop, I would have been quick to search for a kitchen. Lazy consumer that I am, I'd have to be sponsored for charity to even think about walking five miles. Such a route march would be an extraordinary feat in an otherwise sedentary existence. But for the two companions in Luke's story, the seven-mile journey to Emmaus was not a fundraising event but an ordinary, everyday journey. And yet on this particular day, the length of the walk turned out to be about the only thing that was ordinary.

For Cleopas, an ordinary walk begun in a state of mourning and disbelief ended in unprecedented celebration and newness of faith. While the geographic distance was short, this journey from Jerusalem to Emmaus was one of cosmic proportions. Cleopas and his companion are not the only ones to have travelled this road. All who follow Jesus, not to mention creation itself, go this route. It is not simply the private mystical encounter of two travellers two thousand years ago; every disciple since has experienced the Easter journey, from death to resurrection and from darkness to life. What's more, the journey to Emmaus reflects the movement of the planet and human history as a whole. By the end of this first-century road trip, the world had jolted from fallen past towards a perfect future.

In the pages ahead, we will join Cleopas on his short walk to hope. But beware: this kind of hope can induce powerful effects. It can change the world in a minute, turn darkness into light and death into life. What's more, this one true brand of hope, the hope of divine revelation and eternal life, is only to be found in the one whom God raised from the dead. As we retrace Cleopas' steps along the Emmaus road, and occasionally stop to admire the view, we will look to the risen Christ to teach us how to live hopefully ever after.

Don't leave home without it

Who is Cleopas and how did he come to be part of Jesus' band of followers in the first place?

This question is not easy to answer. In terms of the casting of the gospels, Cleopas is nowhere near the top of the bill. Up until this point in Luke's gospel he has figured even less prominently than some of Jesus' female followers which, in male-dominated first-century Palestine, is saying something. However, the fact that the author names Cleopas is significant, for reasons that we will share along the way. For now, it is enough to say that Cleopas was one of Jesus' followers, one of the hopeful band of Israelites who had become captivated by their would-be Messiah. Some time earlier Cleopas, like others, had decided to stop whatever he was otherwise doing and follow Jesus to Jerusalem.

At eighteen years of age, having flunked my auditions for music college, I made a quick decision which would change my life forever. At the time, I was oblivious to the potential long-term consequences of a year out. However Dr Dean, my English teacher, was very aware of them. Singling me out after class, he made me promise that I would definitely go to university following my gap year. The request was not unreasonable. After all, I had no intention of missing out on the subsidized holiday of higher education. And yet, my enthusiastic acceptance failed to dispel his concerns. The next moment, Dr Dean was warning me of the dangers of distraction and pleading with me, in the presence of witnesses, to commit there and then to a three-year university course. With other teachers, it would have been easy to ignore such histrionics. But Dr Dean was different. To those of us who had the privilege of being his students, he appeared to be on a higher plane; he was almost too good to be a teacher. In fact, none of us could work out why he hadn't left teaching. At eighteen years of age, the rest of us couldn't wait to escape school.

'Promise me now that you will go to university!' Dr Dean exclaimed. I'd never heard him raise his voice like this before. Shocked by the outburst I gulped and nodded.

'I promise,' I said.

'Thank the Lord,' he sighed, 'otherwise you'll never learn to cook.'

Dr Dean's passion was not for future learning, nor for the possible loss entailed by the academy in my absence. In all fairness, his concerns also stretched far beyond my prospective culinary skills. He wanted to see me develop as a human being. He desired that I should leave home, become a grown-up, taste the riches of life and learn to rustle up something more nourishing than a microwave ready-meal in the process. As was usually the case, Dr Dean was right and so I followed his instructions to the letter. In fact, I even went the extra mile and took a four-year course.

In the first century, however, teachers, elders and parents did not plead with their sons to leave home. Young adults did not take university courses or gap years. The disciples had most likely grown up in small towns or villages. Many would have had essential roles in their family's business. Rarely travelling far from home, they would have been expected to walk the same streets till the day that they died – that was, until Jesus came along. Until then they were part of the local furniture. They knew everyone, and everyone knew them and their business.

After meeting Jesus, many found their lives thrown into holy disarray. Fishermen left their nets, tax collectors left their booths and many others left familiar surroundings and loved ones. While other rabbis taught from one location, Jesus' followers were enlisted to go on a miraculous mystery tour. And this was only the beginning. The followers of Jesus that the gospels name, such as the disciples, Mary and Martha and Cleopas, represent only a small number of those who had become caught up in Jesus' ministry prior to the crucifixion. But why did they give up house and home, livelihood and loved ones for Jesus? In short, what were they hoping for?

There is nothing to suggest that Cleopas was young. In fact, as we shall soon see, certain theories surrounding his identity would place him as an older gentleman. And yet he, like many others, stopped whatever he was doing, left wherever he came from and followed this radical young rabbi. Why did he leave home? The answer is simple. He left in search of the one thing that everybody looks for and no one can live without. It wasn't career, education, independent living or good food that drew men and women to Jesus. These would-be disciples were convinced that Jesus could show them the one thing for which all Israel was hoping. They were convinced that he could show them the kingdom of God.

Your kingdom come?

Having finally made it to college, I, like many students, found myself going to great lengths to avoid buying or making food. Being part of a church made this challenge considerably easier. Many were the times when I abused Christian fellowship and invited myself to dinner at the houses of different brothers and sisters. My all-time favourite venue for central heating and fine tucker was the home of Isaac and Marietjie (pronounced *mar-ee-kee*). Not only were they two of the kindest, most generous people you could ever meet, but they lived in a swanky apartment in Chelsea overlooking the River Thames. Isaac and Marietjie were South Africans and old family friends of Charlotte, my then girlfriend and now long-suffering wife. In all our visits, Charlotte would address Marietjie as Tannie Marikie. For years I thought that this was her name. Being a polite young man, I never thought to question the strangeness of this double-barrelled Christian name. I just assumed that many women in South Africa were called Tannie something or other. And so, following

Charlotte's lead I simply addressed Marietjie in the same fashion.

When I eventually got to South Africa I discovered that my assumption was only half right. Certainly, many Afrikaans-speaking women are in fact addressed as Tannie something or other. However, the reason for this is that 'Tannie' means Aunty. I then realized that I had been addressing a woman whom I'd known for only a matter of months as though she were my long-lost aunt. Everything suddenly became clear to me – the warm embrace when I walked through the door and the huge helpings of food dished up on to my plate.

As someone who is paid to communicate things, I am continually amazed by my ability to misunderstand and misspeak. Yet, while most people are saved from the regular embarrassment that I seem to pile upon myself, we can all relate to times when we've used words without fully understanding their meaning. In church life, for instance, we can too easily find ourselves lapsing into Christianese. Sadly, few of us think to question the jargon or even ask for clarification. Not wanting to ask a silly question, we simply trust that everyone else knows what we're talking, singing or praying about. Christianity is the message of hope for the world; surely we should always seek to communicate clearly and never reduce it to meaningless cliché.

As a child, I never understood what the phrase 'the kingdom of God' meant. I prayed the Lord's Prayer and asked for God's kingdom to come countless times, yet it never occurred to me ask what was coming and what it would look like when, finally, it came. And still, years later, I was happy to pray for the kingdom in church services, school assemblies and Sunday school but, in truth, I hadn't the foggiest idea what I was praying for. As I read more of the gospels I began to wonder whether Jesus himself knew the answer. Whenever he was asked about it he seemed to change the subject or tell a weird-sounding story. Likewise, when his listeners asked difficult questions or for explanations for his marvellous acts, his answer always had to do with the kingdom, regardless of the question. As I heard one preacher confess, 'It seems that Jesus uses the kingdom to confuse most of the people for most of the time.'

While this confusion over God's kingdom began to cause me disquiet, I remained at peace in the knowledge that someone cleverer than I must have worked it out on my behalf. However, after a while even this consolation wore off. Left with serious and worrying questions, I became almost paranoid. What if no one knew what Jesus was going on about? Might it be possible that the entire church was in the same position as I was? Is the whole Christian community hoping for something that they don't understand? How will we know when God's kingdom finally comes and, more worryingly, what if we've already missed it?

Having taken time to study this question further, I can confirm that there are many who really do know what they are praying for when they ask for God's kingdom to come. What's more, I can enthusiastically promote the benefits that come from time spent exploring the subject in depth. In fact, as Cleopas would confirm, the kingdom really is the only thing worth hoping and praying for. Jesus' followers knew what they were talking about when they discussed the kingdom of God. Far from religious jargon, it was the most topical talking point of their day. While interpretations differed as to how God's kingdom might come about, there was little controversy surrounding its meaning. To talk of the kingdom was to prophesy about, and pray for, a particular day. This day would mark the moment when God would restore his promised rule in Israel, when God would appoint his king and bring about his kingdom.

In the first century, the kingdom was more the object of hopeful thinking than it was present reality. After all, it had been generations since Israel was last ruled by one of her own kings. For centuries she had suffered under the oppressive rule of hostile and pagan regimes. And yet, through this barren time, God's people continued to pray, 'Your kingdom come, your will be done!' And yes, they did pray these very words. By the time of Jesus' incarnation this had become a common Jewish prayer. Since the fall of Jerusalem and her exile in Babylon, Israel had hoped for a time when God would vindicate himself and honour his promise to place one of David's descendants on the throne. While God's promised fulfilment probably felt further off than at almost any time before, this prayerful people tried desperately to keep their hopes up.

Prior to Christ's incarnation, the expectations of God's kingdom had proved almost too much to bear. For too long God's people had raised their hopes to heaven only to watch the sky come crashing down instead. Even the prophets, the mouthiest of God's messengers, had gone quiet. God's people had grown tired. Too often, high hopes had been shattered. Too frequently, Israel's dreams had been dashed. However, at the time of Caesar a strange hiatus occurred. In an attempt to rule the region peacefully, Rome allowed Israel to have a king. And although bully boy Herod was not the nation's ideal choice for a monarch, being ruled by a king of her own was infinitely more attractive than the prospect of being ruled by a pagan. Herod bought favour with his people by rebuilding the temple. This was possibly the only time in history when building work was music to the ears of local residents. For with the temple came the opportunity for sacrifice and prayer, the secret ingredients of Israel's hopefulness.

This peace-offering from Rome was not enough for everyone. First-century Palestine was home to many a dissenting insurrectionist. These revolutionaries hid in the hills and lived to see the downfall of Rome and the installation of God's true king. They saw not only Rome, but also the impostor Herod, as the enemy. While Herod was Jewish, his character was less than kingly and his blood was far from blue. Not born of David's line, he had no rightful claim to the throne. Herod secured his position by his ability to keep his Roman paymasters happy. His merciless attempts to buy favour with Rome, by brutally stamping out uprisings and wilfully killing his own people, kept him in power. While few were happy with this kind of rule, most people assumed that Herod was the better of two evils. In a world where it was illegal to worship any gods but the gods of Rome, Herod's protection racket enabled partial rule and protected the rights of Jews to worship the one true God.

Into this uneasy stand-off stepped Jesus. Reawakening the instincts of a prophetic people, he quickly amassed support and gathered a growing band of followers. His followers placed their faith in him and their hope in his kingdom call. They left homes, jobs and loved ones to follow him. The journey on which Cleopas and the others had started out could have only one destination. They were marching with faith, hope and love towards God's coming kingdom.

Is it nearly here yet?

The Jews thought that the kingdom would come in their time, and Cleopas and co. became convinced that it would come through Jesus.

God has been gracious in giving unto me the spiritual gift of procrastination. Without wishing to be sexist, I have to say that he clearly gives this gift with more frequency to men than to women. Most women I know are far too productive and fruitful to bear the full burden of procrastination. As the verse from Proverbs that I have yet to find but am convinced is there says, God's procrastinators 'rarely put off till tomorrow that which they could do next week'.

As with any spiritual gift, it's no good just scoring high on procrastination in one of those spiritual gift questionnaires; in order for it to be worthwhile one has to use the gift in everyday life. With this in mind, I begin every day with a prolonged time of procrastination. As I lie in bed, having pressed the snooze button on my alarm no less than three times, once for each member of the Trinity, I move into a time of *mathematical procrastination*. In this phase, my mind is beset by endless calculations. How long will it take to get out of bed, have a shower and shave, get dressed, grab breakfast, say goodbye to Charlotte and the kids and get off to work? The computations become increasingly complex as each minute ticks by. Not wishing to get out of bed when I could in fact wait a few minutes longer, I move into a time of *economic procrastination*. I ask myself how I can make the most of the minutes I have left. Ironically, by not shaving I can shave five minutes off my preparation time. If I can wear jeans rather than a suit, I can save another three. If I'm able to grab breakfast at work, grunt at the kids rather than say 'goodbye' and take the short cut, I can delay getting up even longer.

With these exacting calculations complete I move into the final and, some might say, the least logical phase of my early morning procrastinational. However, knowing that God uses the foolish things to expose the wise, I give myself to *punctual procrastination*. This phase relies on the premise that one should not get out of bed unless the last number on the alarm clock is a five or a zero. Hence no faithful procrastinator will get out of bed at 6:32, when they could wait till 6:35. And of course, if you've waited till 6:35 you might as well wait till 6:40. In these final moments we experience the procrastinator's ultimate dream: a kingdom where we can lie in for ever, a new time when we'll never have to get up again.

Only after I have performed the superhuman feats required to make up for those extra minutes in bed can I acknowledge that I will probably never reach this kingdom of eternal lie ins. But I wonder how many of us are guilty of secretly wondering if Jesus' kingdom is so far in the future it will never arrive? When translated into English, Jesus' talk of the kingdom can appear overly futuristic. In his rendition of the gospel story, Matthew always refers to the kingdom of *heaven*. Some of us have taken this kingdom of heaven language to mean that the kingdom is situated at the end of time. The kingdom of heaven happens the day after our furthest tomorrow. It is a time beyond time, a kind of parallel dimension, entirely independent from our universe and what we know in the here and now.

However, while Jesus' followers knew that the kingdom was different from their present experience, they did not think of it as some unknown reality on the other side of time and space. The kingdom of God did not lie somewhere over the rainbow, way up high. Because God promised the kingdom to Israel, their hope for God's kingdom was a historical hope. When he asks for God's kingdom to come, Cleopas is not looking forward to pie in the sky when he dies but rather demanding steak on his plate while he waits. For in the same way that Israel's history was testimony to God's ability to identify and appoint a king, her future relied on his promise of a king to come. There was a reason why Herod's namesake and predecessor massacred infants at the time of Christ's birth. Even this ungodly individual expected God to intervene and appoint a rightful heir to Israel's throne. Fearing that this was about to take place, Herod sought to prevent the promised divine intervention by wiping Jesus from the face of the earth. Fortunately the assassination attempt failed and so, while an entire generation of male sons was tragically lost, the one male Jew who could save every generation was saved.

Jesus' life demonstrates exactly how God's kingdom enters into human history. What's more, his signs and stories made this hope real. These were not the stuff of science fiction or escapist fantasies. His ministry was a dramatic real-life documentary recording God's desire and determination to act in human history. Jesus' followers were fascinated by how God would work in their here and now. For too long, our ignorance of God's kingdom and our consequent tendency to push it into the future have made us into procrastinators where the kingdom is concerned. When we push the kingdom into the far-flung reaches of the future, we don't have to worry about what it means for today. In fact, if we locate God's hope in another time entirely, we can get off the hook where our responsibility to the present is concerned.

God's kingdom is our wake-up call, but most of us respond by hitting the snooze button again and again. It can't really be God's kingdom, because that's not coming till tomorrow. Most of our prayers for God's kingdom to come contain no urgency or expectation. Tomorrow is always a day away. It never comes.

Those Jews who first chose to follow Jesus were not looking for life beyond the grave, a time beyond time. They were convinced that God could and would act in their own history. Where they were concerned, if anyone was asleep it was God. Wide awake, they daily attempted to raise their Creator by shouting 'Your kingdom come!' to the heavens.

As Cleopas set out for Emmaus, he carried with him a broken heart and a busted hope. He and his friends had walked with Jesus and felt sure that the kingdom was at hand. Indeed, Jesus had gone so far as to entrust his kingdom power with his disciples. He told them, 'As you go, preach this message: "The kingdom of heaven is near." Heal the sick, raise the dead, cleanse those who have leprosy, drive out demons' (Mt. 10:7–8). In Jesus and his disciples, it appeared that God was ready, waiting and wanting to enact his will in the world. His power was real and available, so much so that God enabled the disciples to perform mighty acts for the sake of God's kingdom. And yet as Cleopas set out Jesus was dead and buried, his kingdom vanquished and his power put out.

Are we nearly there yet?

When it comes to finding a place to live in hope and happiness, or so estate agents are fond of telling us, there are only three rules: Location, location, location. The hopes of first-century Jews for God's impending kingdom centred on one location: Jerusalem, Jerusalem, Jerusalem. Along with Jesus' other followers, Cleopas not only expected God's kingdom to arrive in a certain time, but in this certain place. While the time of God's kingdom was wrapped up in Jesus' coming, the location of the kingdom concerned where Jesus was going.

As a dad, I regularly drive my kids to the magical land of *There*. *There* is a miraculous place. It is nowhere and yet everywhere. Every time we get into the car, whether we are going on a family outing, our summer holiday or a trip to the shops, my sons will sing an old folk song beloved by children everywhere. 'Are we nearly *There* yet?' they chant over and over until I wish that I'd taken the car salesman up on the optional rear ejector seats. For my kids, it doesn't matter where *There* is. It can be five or five hundred miles away. For them, *There* is all important because the expectation of arrival overrides all fun in the journey.

For Jesus and the disciples, the kingdom is a reality not only in their own time but also in their own space. As they journeyed with Jesus their hopes for God's kingdom flourished. Likewise, as the weeks went by, they became more convinced that Jesus was leading them towards the obvious geographical location of God's kingdom. In the weeks before Christ's passion, we can almost hear them asking, 'Are we nearly *There* yet?' It was no coincidence that Jesus directed his earthly journey towards Jerusalem. For the Jews, Jerusalem was the epicentre of the universe, the meeting point between heaven and earth. If God's kingdom was to come to the world, it would start *There*.

As Jesus and the disciples approached Jerusalem in the weeks before his death, the pace of their journey quickened

and expectations grew. Concerns for Jesus' safety led some
to worry that they might not make it *There* alive. But their
relief upon arrival was short-lived. With Jesus' entry into
Jerusalem on Palm Sunday, the narrative speeds ahead
again. For a moment there was triumph and celebration but
this soon turned to confusion and outrage. Moments after
his victorious entry into the city, Jesus was turning over
tables in the temple and turning on his own people.
Shouldn't he be attacking Israel's Roman oppressors rather
than their God-given religious institutions? Then the Last
Supper, Judas' betrayal, Jesus' prayer in the garden and,
finally, his arrest and trial. As the world seemed to spin out
of control the disciples faced the full reality of God's coming
kingdom in their own time and space. If this was it, it was
not turning out as they expected.

Walking away

The story is told of three British soldiers who stumbled
through the square of a small French village. It was finished.
They had arrived at the end of the road. Anguished cries
gave way to eerie silence. Thoughts of victory were stunted
by sheer disbelief. Was it really over? Had they really won?
Clutching half-empty bottles of wine, they swaggered and
swayed to the sound of their own inebriated interlude.
Pausing for rest, they leaned against the large wooden doors
of a church, only to fall headlong into the building. As their
curses invaded this sacred space, one of the soldiers spied
the confessional booth and staggered towards it. The
onlooking priest dutifully rose and took up his seat alongside. The soldier did his best to turn the air blue and the

priest's face red. His phoney confession was a boasting session. He wallowed in his own depravity, regaling him with tales of drunkenness and debauchery, pride and promiscuity. He fully expected, even desired, to be ejected from the church – but not in the way it turned out.

'I want you to get up and leave my church,' the priest began, 'but before you do, I would ask that you do one thing.' Startled by his calm response and command of English, the soldier listened. 'Before you leave, I would like you to walk to the high altar, look up at the statue of Christ on the cross and repeat these words. "Jesus, I know who you are and I know what you've done for me and I don't give a damn!"' The soldier half fell out of the booth and lurched towards the altar. There he looked up and began. 'Jesus!' he screamed, 'I know who you are and I know what you've done for me . . .' He broke off mid-sentence and stared down at his feet. After what seemed like an age he lifted his head to the cross and started again but this time his voice was quieter, less enraged. 'Jesus, I know who you are,' he began. 'And I know what you've done for me and . . . I am so, so sorry.'

Cleopas knew what it was like to have the image of a dying Christ etched into his imagination. The thought of Jesus on that cross must have haunted him all the way along the road. Whether he felt any responsibility for Jesus' death is impossible to say. What is certain is that on this morning, as he ambled along, he must have made a sorry sight. Cleopas' pain may have been even more personal. Certain contemporary scholars have identified Cleopas as the Clopas of John's gospel (Jn. 19:25). Clopas, who is mentioned only once, was the husband of Mary's sister. His companion on the road that morning may well have been his wife, one of the women who had also watched Jesus die only hours earlier. If Cleopas was Jesus' uncle, he would have known Jesus for far longer than the other followers. He would have known of the events that surrounded his birth and watched him grow from an innocent child into the wisest of men. This was not simply the latest could-be Messiah he had followed into Jerusalem. This was a member of his own family. One who he had believed carried the hopes of the world on his shoulders. Unlike the British soldiers, Cleopas knew nothing of victory. Whatever war he thought Jesus might rage, was surely lost. Faith, hope and love had been fatally defeated. The one in whom he had placed his hope would never vanquish the Romans, expose Herod or receive a throne in Jerusalem. It is impossible for us to begin to grasp the proportions of Cleopas' devastation. Jesus was dead, and the kingdom was gone. Having invested his hope in Jesus, Cleopas was now bankrupt.

'Have you ever had a big investment go south?' a friend recently asked me. I had to confess that I hadn't. Apart from my house and pension, I'm not sure I have anything that would count as an investment. James proceeded to tell me how he'd been conned into parting with thousands by someone he trusted, only to see his money disappear and his friend thrown into prison. He has every right to feel sorry for himself.

Having given up house and home, jobs and livelihoods, Jesus' followers had invested everything they had in the hope of God's imminent kingdom. They did it all in good faith and with great hopes. They believed that their sacrifices would be dwarfed by the kingdom they were about to inherit. Jesus intimated as much when he said, 'Everyone who has left houses or brothers or sisters or father or mother or children or fields for my sake will receive a hundred times as much and will inherit eternal life' (Mt. 19:29). And yet, with Christ's crucifixion, all this hope appeared lost.

Like soldiers at the end of a war, one could almost have forgiven Cleopas had he drowned his sorrows and cursed his God. But he didn't. As he stepped out along the Emmaus road, Cleopas was left to consider the absolute price of Christian discipleship. He'd given everything he had to follow Jesus and watched everything he hoped for die with him on the cross. Like every true follower since, Cleopas' discipleship began with bankruptcy. He had nothing to offer God or the world save his willingness to walk with Jesus.

I remember vividly the moment when the cost of discipleship first dawned on me – at the beginning of my year out, that period between school and learning how to cook at college. In a moment of uncharacteristic clarity I came to the recognition that following Jesus might require me to relinquish the plans that family, teachers and others had made for me. I had to accept that the way to God's kingdom might lead me to live in a neighbourhood that I didn't want to live in, to do a job that wasn't what I'd dreamed of or to be part of a local church that wouldn't meet all my needs. While it sounds melodramatic, the process of abandoning my ambitions and aspirations felt like a mini death. I realized that Christ knew best; I recognized that his was the way to fullness of life; and I believed that the adventure he had in mind was far better than anything I had planned. And yet the idea of abandoning my own hopes, no matter how trifling or unimpressive they seemed, appeared unbearable. Like Cleopas and countless others since, this experience taught me that the hopeful journey which Christ leads us on begins only when we, realizing what Christ gave up on the cross, relinquish our own selfish hopes.

For Cleopas, these hopes included his preconceived ideas of God's kingdom. The key ingredient of this hope was a change of regime in Jerusalem with a rightful heir on the throne, be it by divine intervention or revolution. Maybe he also dreamed of securing a position of influence in the courts of a newly crowned king. Whatever his hopes, the events of Good Friday had forced him to leave them by the wayside. Note that none of these would have seemed ungodly at the time. To wish for God to act and to save his people was hardly a crime or vice. And yet, for Cleopas, the road to hope begins at the point when he is forced to relinquish his own mistaken assumptions about who Jesus was and what he might do for him. The pain of the cross for Jesus' followers was not only the loss of their friend but also the loss of their hopes. Through it all they learned one fundamental truth, namely that God often bears little regard to how we think he should act. Even for those of us who know the end of the story and understand all that we have to gain, the prospect of forfeiting our own well-laid plans can be painful. But as Jesus himself warned, 'Whoever finds his life will lose it, and whoever loses his life for my sake will find it' (Mt. 10:39).

After two years of preparation, it was within our reach – a project that many had said would never happen was about to leap into life. This was huge. Just imagining the impact of the initiative was electrifying. Personally, this was it. The challenge I had been waiting for. The ministry I had been created for. And then it happened. After all that time, energy, passion and prayer, the project stalled, never to start again. I was heartbroken. No amount of prayer could bring it back to life and no number of debriefings could provide solace. For a period I was angry. After all, this wasn't just a silly, selfish pipedream. I wasn't a naive adolescent planning to become a pop star. My hope was godly. All I wanted to do was to try and change a community, to see God's kingdom come. Surely that's one hope I could keep. After a while, there came a point when I needed to put broken hopes and dreams to one side and walk away. You see, there's no point resting in grief when Jesus has a way to resurrection. And yet, if we wish to find this resurrection hope, we must first be prepared to leave our own hopes at his cross. In time, like Cleopas, we may find our old hopes renewed, expanded, altered and even transformed. In the meantime we must be willing to die to even our most 'godly' hopes if we are to discover the true hope of God's kingdom.

Long live the King!

As Cleopas set out along the Emmaus road he contemplated the death of Jesus and the possible death of hope itself. Little did he know that real hope, an eternal hope that is immune to death, was just around the corner.

I remember reading of a well-known charity that had been hustled out of several million pounds. The thought of so many people giving generously to this organization, some at great personal cost, only to have their hard-earned money robbed by unscrupulous conmen, was awful. The press had a field day, inflicting yet more discomfort and tarnishing the organization's reputation. Unfortunately, the media largely ignored the story's happy ending. Good news is often no news to editors and TV news directors. Months after the crime, the police recovered every penny. What's more, the charity's insurance company reimbursed the lost interest. All this meant that the charity received more money back than they had lost in the first place. Just when things looked hopeless, God stepped in and snatched victory from the jaws of defeat.

Jesus' followers wanted to see Jesus crowned as the king of God's kingdom on earth. They were hoping for a coronation, not an execution. They watched Jesus' triumphant entry into Jerusalem, only to see defeat snatched from the jaws of victory. What Cleopas and the others had yet to realize, however, was that Christ's crucifixion was not a defeat. Although it appeared to be the most humiliating event in history, Christ's crucifixion marked his finest hour. In his perfect obedience to the Father's will, in his refusal to turn away or call down angels to rescue him, Jesus showed his true colours. In his determination not to give in to torture, in his words of welcome to a common criminal and in his willingness to forgive the priests, crowds, rulers and soldiers who had put him there, we witness the endless mercy of God in action.

The cross of Christ provides the perfect picture of who the Creator is. If we want to identify the one God who made the heaven and the earth, we can do no better than to look at the one who hangs on the cross and says, 'Father, forgive them.' To call this moment a defeat is to miss the point of the event. John's gospel poignantly portrays the cross as the very throne of God. By demonstrating, once and for all, his absolute willingness to serve the world, Jesus is exalted above all creation. It may not look like the kind of exaltation that Cleopas and friends were expecting, but then Jesus had made a habit of confounding convention and expectation – often quite dramatically. Unlike worldly heirs, Jesus was not looking for a bejewelled and golden crown; he was pleased to wear a crown of thorns. Reared not in a prince's palace but in the home of a carpenter, he knew that precious metals were not essential materials for a throne. A few bits of wood and a handful of nails would do. Those who plotted his defeat by public execution only served to orchestrate his coronation. Even the sarcasm of the Golgotha signage backfired. For under that very inscription Jesus was crowned King of the Jews. In fact, as he hung with his arms open to all, Jesus became King of the world.

In days to come Cleopas would rehearse the events of Good Friday in the light of the revelation of Christ's resurrection. The hindsight that the coming hours and days would provide transformed his horror into hope. On that Friday, Jesus had not only fulfilled the expectations of his followers – he had far surpassed them. However, as he began his journey, Cleopas was far from this declaration.

As the soldier walked the road away from the small French church on that cold winter's evening, he knew what Cleopas was yet to discover. The hope of humankind is not to be found in one who can cheat or avoid death but rather in the power of God to confront death. Possibly the greatest miracle of Jesus' life was his willingness to die for the very people who wanted him dead. As the soldier stared into the eyes of the crucified Christ, the sacrifices of his friends and countrymen found some meaning. More importantly, he discovered fresh hope in the eyes of one who had made the ultimate sacrifice.

A while back I had the privilege of talking to one of those clever chaps who knows more than most about God's kingdom. What surprised me was the honesty of his confession. He too, it turns out, had been slow to grasp the importance of God's kingdom. After a near lifetime of praying the Lord's Prayer every day, and often several times a day, it had only recently dawned on him that we are meant to pray 'Your kingdom come,' as though we mean it.

In the same way that we can't simply push it in to the future, neither can we limit God's kingdom to the past. The fact that Jesus was crowned on a cross two thousand years ago does not mean that his kingdom has been and gone. As the risen Christ, he continues to reign. Hence God's kingdom has as much to do with our world now as it did in Cleopas' time. As a result, when we pray, 'Your kingdom come,' we must be ready to see Christ's kingship take hold in the here and now. We must expect him to surprise us, to show up and mess us up. By proclaiming him king, we invite him to assert his authority over our lives, families, churches and communities. Most of all, we look forward to seeing how his plans and purposes will come to pass in and through us.

There is a reason that we call the Friday of Easter 'Good'. As a result of these surprising and shocking events, human beings find reason to hope. There we find the strength to walk through grief, the wherewithal to imagine a different future and the power to believe in the gritty yet awe-inspiring reality of God's kingdom. In short, we need the cross. For at the cross we can put down our worst failings, most terrible fears, deepest inadequacies, highest ambitions and greatest hopes. We can safely leave these things in the trusted and scarred hands of Jesus because he died so we can live. Good Friday was 'good' because of Sunday – the cross and the tomb are empty and we proclaim, 'Long live the King!' However, for now, we return to Cleopas as he trudges along the Emmaus road in confusion and despair.

2

Hope After Death

The road ahead

In this chapter we will explore the hope of resurrection. As we join the travellers on their way to Emmaus, we discover that rumours of resurrection abounded. Jesus' sermons, stories and signs had stirred up expectations among a people who had long anticipated God's intervention. And yet, no one could have predicted what this would actually look like. When Jesus joined Cleopas on his journey to Emmaus their discussion got off to an uncomfortable start. As Jesus quizzes Cleopas on the events of Good Friday we witness the unique way in which the Easter story brings hope even in the face of death. Having come to the conclusion that all hope was lost, Cleopas began to see that his original hopes were far bigger than he'd imagined. In a little town called Emmaus we discover that the community we call the church has shown, and continues to show, that the good news of resurrection is more than a rumour.

They were talking with each other about everything that had happened. As they talked and discussed these things with each other, Jesus himself came up and walked along with them; but they were kept from recognizing him.

He asked them, 'What are you discussing together as you walk along?'

They stood still, their faces downcast. One of them, named Cleopas, asked him, 'Are you only a visitor to Jerusalem and do not know the things that have happened there in these days?'

'What things?' he asked.

'About Jesus of Nazareth,' they replied. 'He was a prophet, powerful in word and deed before God and all the people. The chief priests and our rulers handed him over to be sentenced to death, and they crucified him; but we had hoped that he was the one who was going to redeem Israel. And what is more, it is the third day since all this took place. In addition, some of our women amazed us. They went to the tomb early this morning but didn't find his body. They came and told us that they had seen a vision of angels, who said he was alive. Then some of our companions went to the tomb and found it just as the women had said, but him they did not see.'

He said to them, 'How foolish you are, and how slow of heart to believe all that the prophets have spoken! Did not the Christ have to suffer these things and then enter his glory?' (Lk. 24:14–26)

Dead beginnings ...

Graham was queuing with Brian, a renowned speaker, at a conference centre coffee bar. A man and a woman just in front of them were laughing raucously. Graham recognized them and introduced the speaker to this pair, Andy and Gemma.

'So,' Brian asked, 'how do you two know each other then?'

After a moment of uncomfortable and embarrassed silence Andy and Gemma looked at one another and, in perfect unison, answered, 'We used to be married.'

Like most public speakers, Brian is rarely at a loss for words. In fact, Brian's mouth is powered by a highly charged motor. And yet there in that queue, for what was possibly the first and last time, he was speechless. Of all the questions he could have asked – 'Are you enjoying the con-ference?' 'Is the coffee any good?' 'Do you come here often?' – he chose to ask a not long divorced couple how they knew each other.

Convention and courtesy often set down tight rules as to what we should talk about and what can be said. In one famous sitcom, an English hotelier hosts a group of Germans only to keep reminding his staff, 'Don't mention the war!' Most of us don't need to be warned about these protocols. We keep complex mental lists of topics to be avoided in certain company. With one of my eco-warrior friends it's a well-known TV show about the motor indus-try. For some it's ex-boyfriends or girlfriends, George Bush, Tony Blair or Rupert Murdoch. In my case, I'd rather not be reminded of a whole string of embarrassing moments, shameful incidents or opera. All of us, there are some sub-jects we'd rather avoid. And, for most of us, death is just one of those topics.

Although being joined by a stranger along the road was not exceptional – in the first century travellers would fre-quently band together to enjoy a safer and more sociable jour-ney – the subject of the conversation was more surprising. When the undercover Jesus enquired as to the topic of their discussion, Cleopas was shocked by his apparent ignorance and proceeded to tell Jesus about his own crucifixion. But why would Jesus feign ignorance or even want to be remin-ded of all of this? What could Cleopas tell him that he didn't know already? Before we become concerned about Jesus' mental state, I should point out that he was not suffering from shock-induced amnesia. Rather, Jesus was anxious to see that Cleopas correctly understood what had gone before. For, from this point on, the future success of his mission relied on how well Cleopas and others relayed this story. Hence, Jesus' death is not a subject to be avoided. No matter how gruesome the detail, the cross was, and continues to be, a defining topic of Christian conversation.

If Jesus does not avoid the subject of death then neither should we. Although it may be tempting to resist entering into conversations concerning mortality for fear of causing discomfort, offence or embarrassing silences, Christians cannot get away with it. In fact, as we saw in the last chapter, the gospel story demands that we confront the issue head-on. And yet our reticence is perfectly understandable, for no subject messes with our hopes and dreams like death. Post-birth, it's the one thing that every human being is assured of and yet the one thing that no one wants to talk about. As a result, the standard way of dealing with death is to avoid the subject altogether, to live in blissful ignorance and determined denial. Most of us cannot afford to pay a wacky scientist to freeze our corpse until such a time when future technology can resuscitate us, so instead we freeze at the mention of our mortality only to be thawed by a change in the topic of conversation.

If any historical figure could have avoided death, one would think that person should have been Jesus, the one through whom all things were created. What's more, having lived a sinless life, did he not deserve a reprieve due to good behaviour? This idea was not lost on his contemporaries. 'Aren't you the Christ? Why not save yourself?' shouts a fellow on death row. However, the plain fact remains. Jesus didn't avoid death. He didn't activate a divine get-out clause, nor did he cheat his way out of it.

Jesus died. This is one of the most remarkable facets of the Christian story. Jesus chose the most undesirable and yet unavoidable of human destinies for his own. What's more, he not only tasted death himself but swallowed every ounce of it in order to save the world. On the cross, the Bible teaches, Jesus was hit with everything that death could throw at him: human sin and selfishness, cursed and fallen creation, the demonic forces of darkness. All of these were taken out on Jesus as he hung on the cross. And yet, as we discovered in the last chapter, the onlookers at this public execution were not eyewitnesses to God's defeat. Having seen Christ's coronation on the cross, his followers have stood in the throne room of God and they proclaim his victory over death once and for all. God did not overcome death by avoiding it or magicking it away but by facing it. While others may wish to avoid the subject, the gospel shouts it aloud. As Jesus walked along the Emmaus road he made it clear to Cleopas why these things had to happen. As a result of his death and resurrection, there is new hope for humanity and history. The moral of the story is simple: Jesus dealt with death, once and for all.

Andy and Gemma still laugh when reminded how they queued for coffee with Brian. Upon reflection, the story is as poignant as it is humorous. You see, their carefree laughter owed more to the resurrection than anyone will ever know. While many prayed for reconciliation, their marriage had ended. No amount of human hindsight will ever answer all the questions. However, the story has a happy ending. The death of their marriage didn't deter their respective journeys with Jesus. By the power of his resurrection, Jesus came alongside both Andy and Gemma, bringing new hope into a situation that they, and others, had once thought hopeless.

As Cleopas walked the Emmaus road, mourning the death of a friend, little did he know that his own fear of death was about to be removed forever. In quizzing Cleopas about his execution, Jesus prepared him for the good news of the resurrection.

First you see him

My grandmother is Italian, hence we call her Nonna. Like most grandparents, she enjoys telling stories about her grandchildren's escapades to anyone who'll listen. One favourite story concerns the time I got lost in a supermarket in Southend-on-Sea. I was five and on a family shopping expedition in preparation for my aunt's upcoming wedding. So there we were in this supermarket, the grown-ups with their long shopping lists and me with my miniscule attention span.

Now there are two versions of what happened next. While the main points remain the same, the tone of the story changes dramatically according to the narrator. Nonna's retelling takes the form of an emotionally intense melodrama, overflowing with excitement and Latin flair. I am the hero of her story. Apparently, I always was a clever boy. The villain is my mum, who didn't seem at all bothered about my welfare as, being a clever boy, I was bound to turn up somewhere. My mum's rendition is an altogether calmer, I-told-you-everything-would-be-alright account. I am also the hero in her version, for reasons that have already become apparent, and the villain is my Nonna – for overreacting, being highly emotional and Italian. The last accusation is a bit rich as my mum is half Italian and, like all of her siblings, more like her mother than she would care to admit.

Despite their differing emotions and vocal pitch, my Nonna and my mum dealt with my disappearance by asking the same question: 'Where could he have gone to?' Having considered all possible answers to this question, a search party was sent out to secure my return. Having become bored by the delights of Southend High Street and, what's more, being such a clever boy, I found the nearest bridal shop and waited for both the panic stricken and the calm to find me. Without wishing to diminish your estimation of my intellectual capacity, I should confess that it wasn't the right wedding shop. But, nonetheless, the shop assistants dutifully took me in and fed me Smarties until my family found me.

In the days following Jesus' crucifixion, one question haunted his followers: 'Where could he have gone to?' It's a question that, at some point, every human asks about themselves or a loved one. It's more commonly phrased like this: 'What happens when we die?' Underlying this ultimate question is one hope – namely that physical death may not be the end of our life story. Whether out of faith or desperation, Cleopas refused to believe that Jesus' story was over. Having brought him up to speed with the story of the crucifixion, Cleopas eagerly informed the stranger of a certain rumour spread by a group of women who claimed to have seen Jesus. If the rumour was true, Cleopas reasoned, then Jesus might not be dead.

What did Jesus' followers believe about life after death? The Old Testament says surprisingly little about it. Jesus' original followers, therefore, had many more questions than answers. Many thought of the afterlife as being wrapped up in the lives of successive generations. Parents lived on through the lives of their children. In part, this explains why childlessness was considered calamitous. In a family-oriented society a childless couple was economically disadvantaged in this life and absent from the next.

Once when browsing through a Christian bookshop I noticed a book called *It's Not Over 'Til the Barren Woman Sings*. I'm not sure who wrote it, but the cover certainly caught my eye. Clumsy though it may be, the title confirms a crucial aspect of Old Testament faith. Through even her most difficult times, Israel believed that God has the power to bring life out of death. The nation's very existence was testimony to God's power to do this. Sarah and Abraham, Israel's mother and father, had also experienced the pain of childlessness. However, having placed what little hope they had in God, a miracle came to pass and they gave birth to a son, Isaac. This miracle would surely have been enough to confirm God's power and answer their prayers, and yet God's plans and promises went far beyond anything that Abraham and Sarah could have hoped for. In effect, Abraham and Sarah gave birth to a nation. Their offspring outnumber the stars and shine the light of God's revelation upon the whole world. Their offspring comprise God's chosen people and their family tree features many great heroes, the Son of God among them. All of this life came from one elderly, barren couple who didn't feel very much like singing.

With this story for her birthright, eternal hopefulness becomes Israel's constitution. Wherever they find themselves, God's people know that the Creator's life-giving power outweighs the ominous threat of death. With God, all things become possible. Having watched a nation born from a barren womb, Israel continued to discover life in the most unlikely places. As a result, God's people are party to an eternally hopeful suspicion that death may not be the ultimate ending to creation's story.

In the centuries prior to Christ's incarnation, the stakes were raised. Through this period, a succession of brutal regimes violently ruled over Israel. With many Jews willing to fight for their nation, the body count was high and on the rise. Under Roman rule, and with King Herod in place, the skirmishes continued, albeit with less regularity. Each death only tested Israel's hope further. The obvious and ultimate questions were now being asked on a daily basis. What had become of those who died trying to save God's people? What happened to those Jews who were executed under Antiochus IV for keeping God's law? Where were those who were massacred while fighting these godless regimes? After all, many did not have children. Surely God could not allow their story to end this way.

By the first century, Israel was hoping against hope. And yet, when hopelessness might so easily have set in, God's people kept hoping. In fact, it was the enduring hope of God's coming kingdom that led many to follow Jesus in the first place. An example for us all, these hopeful followers held on to God's perfect promise in their own imperfect circumstances.

On the same day that I saw *It's Not Over 'Til the Barren Woman Sings*, I went out to dinner with friends. After much merriment, and with my defences down, we got on to the subject of notable books. 'You'll never guess the book title I saw earlier today!' I cried. The crowd were hanging on my every word. Now I may not know much, but I do know how to tell a funny story. So, enjoying the attention of a captive audience, I stretched the story out. For once, my self-indulgence saved the day. As I went to hit them with the punchline, my eyes met with Jenny's. I froze, mortified by the words about to fall out of my mouth.

For a moment everything happened in slow motion. This left me with precious time enough to haul myself back from

the brink of disaster. 'Doh!' I exclaimed, 'I've gone and forgotten what the book was called!' The white lie was a cue for
many quizzical looks and a good deal of embarrassed
laughter. I was filled with a mixture of shame and relief that
I hadn't delivered the 'killer' line in front of Jenny.

Jenny is one of the most impressive Christians I know.
She and her husband are the type of people I'd like to be like
when I grow up. She brings a level of authenticity and
humility to her discipleship that clowns like me can only
dream about. She works in a difficult job, lives in a tough
part of town, serves the poor in the most sacrificial ways
and loves the ones that most of us find utterly unlovable. A
few days before I launched into my lame joke about a dubious book title, Jenny had had a miscarriage. The thought of
throwing that cheap joke in her face haunts me to this day;
as one friend always tells me, my humour too often gets me
into trouble. But Jenny's story does have a happy ending.
Having lived through difficult pregnancies, emergency
scans, panicked conversations and desperate prayers, Jenny
gave birth to a beautiful baby. And through it all she kept
the difficult job, stayed in the tough part of town, continued
to serve the poor and kept on loving the unlovable. In short,
she kept hoping in God when it would have been easier to
give up. Her faith was not the result of an easy or comfortable present but came out of a determined belief that her
future was in God's hands.

The years prior to Christ's incarnation were among the
hardest in Israel's history. And yet, as we have seen,
through the massacres and the persecutions, the invasions
and the indignities, Israel never stopped praying, 'Your
kingdom come. Your will be done. On Earth as it is in
Heaven.' From Abraham and Sarah onwards, the family of

Israel hoped that their God could overcome death. Caught in the dramatic climax of Israel's history, Cleopas' excitable interest in the rumours of Christ's resurrection suggests that there is still hope. The events of the previous few days had not drowned his belief in God's present power or future hope. While Christ's whereabouts was uncertain, Cleopas had a hunch that it wasn't all over. All his life he'd heard talk of resurrection; he'd also witnessed Jesus' ministry and miracles like Lazarus rising from the dead.

Slumber and sleep

One cold, wet Sunday afternoon before Christmas my eldest son Joe was looking for things to do. The fact that all his toys were 'boring', combined with his mother's insistence that he not watch any more TV, forced us towards creative alternatives. 'I know!' I said. 'Let's write a letter to Father Christmas.' Joe welcomed the idea with some excitement. I made myself a coffee and returned with a pen and stationery to find that Joe had fallen asleep on the sofa. Apparently the idea wasn't that exciting after all. By the time he woke up, I was heading out of the house to run an errand.

'But Daddy,' he pleaded, 'I wanted to write to Father Christmas!' Having garbled the general idea in Charlotte's direction I dashed out, leaving Joe and his mum to compose the letter. When I arrived home some hours later, my wife greeted me with a less than welcoming look. Having handed her the paper and pen, Joe had proceeded to dictate the entire contents of Toys R Us for his mum to write down.

Charlotte spent the rest of the afternoon talking him out of writing the letter so that he wouldn't be disappointed on Christmas day. As I tried to point out, at least the idea had provided an afternoon of non-digital distraction. I'm not sure why, but Charlotte seemed less willing to concede the success of my idea.

While it is one thing to believe that death is not the end, it is another thing entirely to meet the risen Christ on the roadside and have him invite himself for tea. So did Cleopas really expect Jesus to rise from the dead? And what led him to believe that such an event was even possible in the first place? In what were difficult times, one could have forgiven Cleopas, and Israel for that matter, for lowering their expectations. And yet they remained hopeful that God would one day deal with death. In fact, in the same way that a child's wish-list grows longer in the run-up to Christmas, Israel's hope grew both before and during the time of Christ.

By the first century, Israel's hunch that God would one day defeat death had developed into a doctrine. In line with this, growing numbers of Jews held passionately to the belief that God would raise the dead. Until such a time, they maintained, the faithful departed slumbered in Sheol, the place of great levelling. This sleep-like state formed God's waiting room prior to the day of resurrection. On that day, and having finally conquered death, God would resurrect the inhabitants of Sheol. By the time of Christ, Jews were talking about resurrection like never before. Certain groups, such as the Pharisees, were defined in part by their belief in resurrection. On the other hand, other sects such as the Sadducees were known to deny the validity of this particular hope. All in all, the people of Israel were desperate for some prophetic sign or revelation that might finally confirm or deny this hope.

A few years back the International Olympic Committee was about to make a decision regarding the location of the 2012 summer games. London, my home city, was on the shortlist and the capital and much of the country waited with eager anticipation. At the time the announcement was made I was travelling on a London Underground train. When I surfaced, I was desperate to know the result. It was too early for the story to be relayed by headline on the newsstands so I tried to read people's faces to see if their expressions would tell me what happened. Finally, arriving in the British Library where I was working that day, I found a friend and whispered softly in his ear, 'Did you hear the announcement about the games? Did we win?' He smiled and nodded. I was just about to leap up, whoop and holler in celebration when I remembered where I was.

With the debate raging in towns and villages, synagogues and the temple, people who encountered Jesus regularly quizzed him about resurrection. Throughout his ministry we see friends and enemies, followers and detractors seeking confirmation of their hopes and suspicions concerning this hope. People scrutinized Jesus' actions, questions, conversations, sermons and stories for clues about the good news of resurrection. Rich young rulers asked what they must do to inherit eternal life (Mk. 10:17). Teachers of the law asked him the same question to test and categorize him (Lk. 10:25). Sadducees tried to catch him out by asking questions about marriage in heaven (Mt. 22:23). Resurrection was the talk of the town and many identified Jesus as the man who could make some kind of final announcement, one way or the other. Jesus' response to this feverish expectation did little to dampen the fire of Israel's hope and yet, at times, he appeared unwilling to give a straight answer to these questions. His responses can seem cryptic. Is he unsure, coy or simply teasing his audience? But one thing was for sure – as he moved closer to Jerusalem rumours of resurrection crescendoed to a new level.

One of the most evocative of these dialogues occurred following the death of Lazarus. During the wake, Lazarus's sister almost blamed Jesus for her brother's death (Jn. 11:21). For if Jesus had been with them, rather than maintaining a low profile elsewhere, he could surely have healed her brother. However, the delay in Jesus' arrival was deliberate. It is as if he had been waiting for an appropriate time and place to demonstrate the reality of resurrection. Seeking to comfort Martha, Jesus said, 'Your brother will rise again.' In response, Martha was quick to nail her theological colours to the mast. She knew that Lazarus would be raised on resurrection day but she pushed Jesus further. Why not now? 'I know that even now God will give you whatever you ask' (Jn. 11:22).

There at his friend's wake in Bethany, Jesus made the biggest noise to date concerning Israel's great hope. 'I am the resurrection and the life,' he declared before dramatically calling Lazarus from the tomb (Jn. 11:25). With the message given and the miracle complete, talk of resurrection reached fever pitch. The raising of Lazarus forms a stunning object lesson for the hope of resurrection. Although Jesus had sometimes given obscure answers in the past, this event revealed more about resurrection than the Jews could have asked or expected. For, while vindicating those who placed their hope in resurrection, it provided a prophetic signpost of a greater miracle to come. Far from avoiding the subject, Jesus had begun to exceed his followers' hopes and aspirations.

By negotiating him out of an overly extensive Christmas wish-list, Charlotte was trying to teach Joe an important life skill – one that the world forces us to learn along life's way. The way to survive daily life is to have realistic expectations. There's no pointing asking for too much, because we'll only be disappointed. Through all eras and civilizations this simple rule has held sway. However, there have been times when history has played tricks on us, exceeding our expectations and turning general wisdom on its head. Journeying with him from Bethany to Jerusalem and then on to Emmaus, Jesus' followers experienced one such time. Far from shying away from his people's questions and hopes, Jesus answered and fulfilled them in unimaginable measure.

With hindsight, we can see that Jesus' message was simple: Resurrection will happen. It will happen through Jesus. It will happen to Jesus. It will happen soon. Many would have been happy with the first statement. Few, if any, could have expected the second and third. While many hoped for a resurrection day, few believed that they would see such an event in their own lifetime. The resurrection would surely take place on the other side of history, at the end of time. That's why Sheol was so important. If resurrection was a long way off, the dead needed a place to go in between times. And, what's more, surely God could not make resurrection happen through the ministry of one rabbi? Surely it would take more than a carpenter's son armed with a few stories and signs to bring about the ultimate hope of God's people?

Having talked the crucified Christ through his own death, Cleopas then discussed the resurrection with the risen Jesus. In time he, along with disciples everywhere, would come to the stunning confession that resurrection day, far from happening on the other side of time, had actually occurred within human history. Easter Sunday is that day. From that day forward, the reality of resurrection hope was confirmed in the here and now. Put simply, all those who walk with Jesus know that resurrection happens. Throughout the two thousand years since Cleopas stepped out for a stroll, Christians have proclaimed the remarkable truth that we don't have to wait to confirm our hope of resurrection. The evidence of the event is right here and right now in the life of the church, the community founded and sustained by the risen Christ. For this reason, the church adopted a new Sabbath day. The Christian holy day is not a commemoration of God's rest day but rather a celebration of Jesus' resurrection day. The Christian Sabbath is a celebration of the fact that on Easter Sunday Jesus rose from the dead and began to make all things new.

I used to attend a church that had a thing for 'faith teas'. These supposedly miraculous feasts occurred at any given occasion. The idea was simple. Every church member would bring some item of food to share with the brethren, and sistren. Ultimately, the size and scope of the menu was a matter of faith. In faith, we believed it would be a veritable smorgasbord of fine foods and sumptuous delicacies. In faith, we believed that there would be enough to go around. In faith, we believed that there would be enough leftovers to feed the lazy disciples who didn't bring anything. But most of all, in faith, we believed that there would be only one quiche. The only problem with these faith teas was the absence of real faith. Rather than asking individual church members to make their contribution a subject of prayer and fasting, people were given specific instructions as to what flavour crisps, brand of soft drink and type of quiche they were to provide. All in all, it was a sad indictment of the lack of faith in this particular community. I mean, if we couldn't trust God to help us make tea, how could we possibly believe that he might use us to change our community?

In my experience, the church rarely suffers from too much faith or hope. Our expectations in these areas are often painfully low rather than unrealistically high. We tend to suffer from a lack of hope, a lowered sense of what is possible and a diminished expectation of what God might and can do. At times we go even further, informing the Lord that anything he does do had better fit in with our plans, timetable, management, theology and finance. The habit of downsizing our hopes has become our worst enemy. It has made us smaller in every conceivable way. What's more, it has made God smaller. For while rumours abound that he can heal the sick and raise the dead, we have downplayed these hopes so as not to disappoint anyone. Once again, we can learn much from God's people past.

Here we have Israel, in her most troublesome and turbulent of times, hoping against hope, dreaming of resurrection day. What's more we have Cleopas, having just witnessed the devastating event of Jesus' crucifixion, hoping that the rumours might really be true, that today might just be that very day. Here is Cleopas, believing that the empty tomb might in fact be the prelude to the greatest story ever told, the good news for which Israel and all of creation yearns. Though his hope as he walked that road may have been tinged with uncertainty, ours is more certain. We no longer wait anxiously for news of the resurrection day, for we know that Christ has already been raised from the dead and that the age of resurrection has well and truly begun. And since this, the greatest of hopes, has become a reality, our expectations of what Christ can do should be raised sky-high. The first Christmas and Easter have come and gone and, unlike my son Joe, we all got more than we could ever have asked for.

What a difference a Sunday makes ...

For Cleopas, a day which began with questions and confusion, mourning and grief ended with answers and peace, joy and celebration. Later that evening, as Jesus took bread and broke it, the whole of history broke open for Cleopas to see. In that moment he left an old world behind and entered new creation.

As a kid, I had no interest in politics or current affairs. The most annoying time of every day was when Mum and Dad insisted that we switch channels from the kids' programmes to watch the news. Growing up in the 1980s, I remember seemingly endless reports on the Cold War. This period of history was defined by the competing ideologies of East and West, of communism versus capitalism, the US and Western Europe against the Soviet Union and the Eastern Block. TV reports, newspaper headlines, spy novels and Hollywood movies all told the same tale. The irresistible progress of capitalism had come head to head with the apparently immovable force of communism. The world faced two unattractive alternatives: the permanent discomfort of an uneasy stand-off or all-out nuclear war.

Then, one cold Christmas night, the world watched as the most joyous yet surprising scenes played out on our TV sets. For once, it was fun to watch the news. I remember watching as the Berlin Wall, the permanent dividing line between two seemingly irreconcilable worlds, tumbled before our eyes. One scene will remain with me forever. As the cameras zoomed in part of the wall gave way, leaving a small hole. Suddenly a hand plunged through this gap. Seizing the day, an onlooker grasped the protruding hand. The closed fist of enmity was at once replaced with the open hand of friendship. In these moments, the world changed forever.

What was it that made the difference for Cleopas? What sign or statement gave Jesus away and helped his friend to realize that the world had changed forever? Was it a recognizable feature, look, gesture or mannerism that dislodged the scales from his eyes? Maybe it was the hands that gave him away? Did Cleopas, like Thomas later that night, catch sight of the scars as Jesus broke the bread before dinner? Or was it the act itself, the familiar gesture, the regular meal-time ritual which Jesus had made his own? Whatever it was, as Cleopas watched Jesus breaking bread in Emmaus, his eyes were opened.

As with many who have grown up into the Christian faith, I cannot remember one particular moment when I first sensed the presence of the risen Jesus. While I acknowledged him to varying levels over the years, I have always known his presence with me. I have, however, had the privilege on numerous occasions of witnessing others open their eyes to the reality of Jesus in their own lives.

Years ago, I was asked to speak at the London School of Economics. The talk was entitled, 'Jesus, Eric Cantona or Karl Marx: Who's given most to the world?' The title was not of my choosing. However, as a Christian I figured I could speak about Jesus, and as a Manchester United fan I was more than happy to talk about Eric Cantona, one of the finest footballers ever to grace the beautiful game. The problem was Karl Marx. Knowing next to nothing about political theory in general and Karl Marx in particular, I threw myself into research. In all these years I have rarely been so relieved to finish a talk and was never so terrified by the prospect of questions. I prayed to God that no one would raise their hand. Unfortunately, God ignored my prayer. While attempting to locate the emergency exits, just in case the debate on Marx got hairy, I noticed a student at the back of the room with his arm raised. Somewhat reluctantly, I gestured towards him.

'I have one question,' he said. He looked intelligent and I felt scared. 'Where would I find out more about the evidence for the resurrection of Jesus?'

I gave a huge sigh of relief and a wonderful discussion ensued. For those interested in the answer to this question, there is much in the way of evidence for the resurrection of Jesus. And yet, above it all one piece of evidence stands out. The very existence of the church, today and through history, is inexplicable other than as a result of the resurrection.

To see this close up we need only look at Cleopas and co. The transformation triggered in those closest to Jesus over the Easter weekend is dramatic, to say the least. There is no record of Cleopas or any other of Jesus' male followers being at the cross. The gospel writers only record women as named eyewitnesses of Jesus' crucifixion. In a society which first and foremost recorded the men present at historical events and which did not consider women to be reliable witnesses, the absence of male names infers that there were none. The one possible deduction is that Jesus' male friends and followers were too scared to attend his execution.

The point is borne out by Peter's behaviour prior to the event. Only hours after Jesus' arrest, this petrified disciple, the one whom Jesus had called 'the rock', wobbled.

Knowing that Jesus was innocent, Peter remained scared that others might judge him guilty by association. As a result he disowned Jesus, claiming that he didn't even know him. With Jesus sentenced to death, the rest of the disciples ran in fear for their lives and hid away. And yet, within a matter of months, these same quivering wrecks were pioneering one of the fastest-growing, longest-living movements in history. What's more, most of them ended their days as death-defying martyrs. The explanation for this transformation is clear. The resurrection of Jesus changed their lives. It was *the* pivotal event. Having encountered the risen Christ, the disciples never faced the same fear again.

I have long loved Tim Burton's film *Big Fish*. For those who haven't seen the movie, the story features a father and his son. No matter how many times I see it, I still laugh at the funny bits and cry with the sad bits. At the end, I do both simultaneously. The main protagonist lives life with great courage and delightful abandon. Quick to live the dream, he seems unperturbed by fear or failure. The secret of his conquering confidence is simple. He knows how he will die. Knowing how his life will end enables him to ride through many a trial and much turmoil. When others suffer mortal fear, he presses on knowing that this is not the end of his story.

The resurrection is not only the happy ending of Jesus' life story; it is also a promise of how his followers' lives will end. His resurrection answers Israel's ultimate question and confirms their greatest hope. Centuries earlier another prophet, Ezekiel, was taken by God to a valley of dry bones. As Ezekiel stood in the festered, unclean remains of his people Israel, God asked him this question: 'Can these bones live?' As Robert Jenson points out, this one question runs through all Old Testament faith. What's more, as we mentioned at the beginning of this chapter, it is the same ultimate questions that all humans ask: 'Is there life after death?' As Jesus broke bread and Cleopas' eyes were opened, the answer to this ultimate question was staring him in the face. In the risen Jesus, Cleopas saw the future of the world. In front of his very eyes sat the ultimate hope of humanity, the happy ending of all history.

In the same way that we watched in near disbelief as the Berlin Wall began to crumble, Cleopas watched the world change before his very eyes. He witnessed divine history in the making. Jesus had finally broken down the wall which stood between life and the afterlife. Reality was no longer to be viewed as two opposing states, life versus death. The hands that broke bread had already defeated death and bore the scars to prove it. From this moment on Cleopas could only live in two possible states – life in the here and now or life eternal. The hope which certain Jews didn't dare to even hope for had come to the town of Emmaus. From this point on, Cleopas knew that his life would not end in death but in resurrection. With this question answered, death lost its sting and the fears of Christ's followers' were removed. From this point onward, they knew how their story would end. No longer bound for death, they hoped for resurrection. Whatever was to come, be it pain or persecution, mourning or martyrdom, Cleopas could begin to live hopefully ever after.

A resurrection people

'Today is the first day of the rest of your life.' As a boy I remember one particular minister who seemed to finish every other sermon with this somewhat hackneyed cliché. However, the problem with clichés is that they usually ring true. This one certainly does as far as our traveller is concerned. For while the evening in Emmaus marked the end of the first Easter weekend, it was only the beginning of a whole new story for Cleopas. The gospel story is never ending; it lives on in the eternal communion of Christ and his church. The Christian church is the family born out of Christ's resurrection. We are a living confession of the one who was dead and yet now lives forever more. As it did for Cleopas and our other forefathers, this news should make us into the most hopeful community on earth. Our hopes and dreams, aspirations and expectations should stretch beyond the stars. Our lives and congregations should provide certain evidence of Jesus' resurrection hope.

In my work for The Salvation Army I spend a good deal of time working with the church to serve young people in deprived communities. Even in the relative prosperity of the UK, it never fails to shock me how early death can take hold of a young life. I'm not talking about the few young people who fall victim to gun crime, although this is part of the story. In the main, I'm talking about the many young people who, by the age of fifteen, have already fallen out of education, suffer from chronically low self-esteem and have no belief in the possibility that their lives could count for something. Cursed by generational unemployment, dysfunctional families and dangerous addictions, they have already exchanged youthfulness for hopelessness. And, as we have said from the start, you can't live without hope. However, while some are happy to write them off, Jesus says different.

Whether the problems are physical, spiritual, social or intellectual, the gospel demands that we confront the dead and the dying with the good news of the resurrection. Whether early or late, expected or unexpected, Jesus breathes his Spirit into us so that we might scream hope to the world. Whether it's a dead relationship or a dying community, a victim of terminal illness or the thousands dying in the developing world, we, God's people, know that death is not the end. Having met the risen Jesus we have seen, first-hand, that resurrection is the happy ending of this world's story. At the end of history, Christ promises us the death of death and the beginning of many hopeful ever afters. The challenge to Christians everywhere is to make this good news known. The challenge to our churches is to demonstrate the resurrection life which makes the church possible in the first place. So let's ask the question: In the same way that first-century seekers saw the early church as hard evidence for the risen Christ, can the same be said of us?

Years before the fall of the Iron Curtain, a group of British pastors visited some of their counterparts in Berlin. During their tour of the city they were taken to a particular point along that enormously divisive wall. The German pastors shared how, at the same time every week, they gathered at this place to pray that God would bring down the wall and bring new hope to his people. That said, they stopped to pray once more. While impressed by their faithfulness, one of the British pastors could not help thinking that the exercise was somehow futile. How could their prayers be powerful enough to bring down this demonic dividing line, this oppressive regime? You can imagine the shock and excitement that surged through that pastor when, some years later, sitting at home on New Year's Eve he watched as people from both sides of the city began to break down the wall. What's more, as the camera zoomed in to a part of the wall, something felt strangely familiar. This was the place where those pastors had held their weekly vigil. The pastor watched as a burly East Berliner wielded and swung his sledgehammer on that same spot. After many blows, part of the wall crumbled – leaving that hole through which one countryman could take the hand of another. It wasn't so much that the German pastors were more faithful than their British counterparts, although that might well be the case. The point is that God's hope transcends all of our attempts at hopefulness.

In his death and resurrection, Jesus exceeds all human hoping. Cleopas could never have imagined that God would answer his nation's prayer in this way. The thought that he would see the resurrection in his own lifetime, let alone at tea time, would have been simply too much to hope for. However, those of us who are part of the church, post-resurrection, know differently. We know that our prayers are not hopeful wish-lists sent heavenwards. We know that our lives are not meaningless accidents heading irretrievably towards the grave. Rather, it is God's Holy Spirit who powers our prayers and our lives – the same one who raised Christ from the dead. As a result, we stand against death and hopelessness and live to assure the world that Christ's resurrection is more than the stuff of religious rumour and wishful thinking. Like Cleopas, we have seen the end of the story and are learning to live hopefully ever after.

3

Hope Before Life

The road ahead

In this chapter we will explore God's hope for creation. Having heard Cleopas share the story of his crucifixion and the earliest rumours of his resurrection, Jesus interrupted and set the record straight with an exposition of the whole Bible. For, in the same way that the Bible makes sense of Jesus' story, so too Jesus makes sense of the Bible's story. From the beginning of human history, God's plan hinged upon Jesus.

As we rehearse the story of creation, three aspects will stand out. Firstly, God's creation is dynamic. Just as Cleopas and co. are travelling towards Emmaus, creation is also moving towards its fulfilment in God. Secondly, God's creation takes time. In the same way that it takes time for the travellers to reach their destination, so too God takes time to achieves his purposes in creation. Thirdly, God has a future for creation. Just as Cleopas' day ends hopefully, the story of creation will end happily ever after.

Finally, in this chapter we'll reflect upon the importance of Jesus' death and resurrection for the whole of creation. Although the events of Easter are fresh in Cleopas' memory, God's decision to save the world was part of an ancient plan. Because they have witnessed the resurrection, the implementation of this divine strategy will soon rest with Cleopas and the others who will walk with Jesus in days to come.

> And beginning with Moses and all the Prophets, he explained to them what was said in all the Scriptures concerning himself (Lk. 24:27).

Back to go

As Jesus took bread and broke it, he confirmed, fulfilled and extended Cleopas' greatest hopes beyond his wildest dreams. And yet, while this meal marked a long-awaited dawn for God's people, the hope that God might overcome death was as old as the hills. So where in the world did hope begin?

Having heard the story of his death and rumours of his resurrection, Jesus resisted the temptation to immediately reveal himself. This can't have been easy. I, for one, find it difficult to stop myself from sharing exciting news. A few friends recently organized a surprise day out for our workmates. While I did manage to keep the secret from my colleagues, I must have told just about everybody else I know what was about to happen. How Jesus did it, I'll never know. But he managed to stop himself from kicking off the big reunion right there and then on the road to Emmaus. Furthermore, Jesus resisted any urge to mop Cleopas' worried brow. While Cleopas was clamouring for a word of consolation, a prophetic promise that things would turn out okay, Jesus resisted the urge to give him any immediate assurance about the future.

Instead of pressing *fast forward*, Jesus rewound to the beginning of time. As we saw at the end of the last chapter, there would be plenty of time for Jesus to relay what will happen at the end of history. At this point, Jesus was anxious to show them the first dawn of hope. And it clearly made an impact, for within minutes Cleopas and co. are captivated by this mobile teaching slot. 'Beginning with Moses', Jesus 'explained to them what was said in all the Scriptures concerning himself' (Lk. 24:27). At this point it is important to note that the Jews had credited Moses with the authorship of Genesis. By using this phrase, then, Luke is informing us that Jesus' teaching session began at the very beginning of the Bible. It seems that Jesus was planning to use this relatively short journey to lead his friends on a walk through the entire Old Testament.

A friend and I were once given the task of teaching a few hundred young teenagers the entire Bible over the course of four mornings. To keep our audience conscious, let alone engaged, was obviously going to be a challenge and so we planned what must have been the single most creative teaching programme that I have ever been involved in. Having done all that work, we felt that we deserved to have some fun at our audience's expense. On the very first morning we began by asking every young person to stand as our guest teacher entered the room. A rather stern and old-fashioned looking character dressed as a teacher wove his way through the slightly bemused crowd. Having taken the stage, this cane-wielding, tweed-wearing old schoolmaster held up his Bible and welcomed the congregation to *The Bible in One Week*.

'Please open your Bibles,' he instructed, 'and turn to page one.' From the side of the stage I could see hundreds of shocked young people who, for that one minute at least, believed we would systematically read through every word together.

In his bid to explain himself and the hope that he brought, Jesus insisted that Cleopas and his companion return to Genesis page one. The implications of this are colossal. Jesus clearly saw himself to be the fulfilment of Old Testament revelation. If we wish to know who God is and become an agent of his hope in the world, we must first meet the risen Jesus and listen to his story. To hear this tale in full we must take in the whole Bible and, what's more, we must hear it the right way round. We begin with a man called Jesus who was born in Bethlehem and raised in Egypt and Nazareth as the son of a carpenter. He became a rabbi, cared for the poor and the outcasts, captivated crowds with his teaching, trained his disciples and performed many miraculous signs – only to suffer public execution. After having been dead for three days, he rose again in order to rejoin his friends and restore and fulfil the hope of creation. This revelation is the platform from which we can tell the rest of the Bible story. For this reason, a truly Christian rendition of God's hope should start with the rising of the Son.

A few years ago I found myself on holiday in Ibiza, an island famous for its bars and nightclubs. Still scarred from my expulsion from the Morris dancing display team at nursery school and, what's more, being white, English and male, I am always reluctant to get overly involved with anything approaching the boogie. Consequently, I expended my limited reserves of energy on the occasional jog, or should I say plod, along the beach. One evening, while out plodding, I found myself running through the Café del Mar. For the uninitiated, this seaside bar is where many an evening's entertainment begins. Hundreds of clubbers gather here for chilled drinks and mellow tunes but, most of all, to watch the sunset. The view from the Café del Mar is entrancing and idyllic. In the early evening, the sun forms a perfect orange sphere above the stilled blueness of the Mediterranean ocean. Then, in one breathtaking minute, this great ball of orange fire melts into the cool evening sea. After the sun sets, the crowd joins in the most amazing ovation.

As I lurched along the shoreline, dripping in sweat and collecting bemused looks from the assembled partygoers, I caught sight of this sunset and stopped. As the crowds clapped and cheered, whistled and hollered, I found myself deeply moved. While the clubbers welcomed the darkness with the night that had just begun, another thought came to my mind. In a few hours, the sun would rise again and herald the dawn of a new day. In that weird and wonderful moment, it occurred to me that the entire story of our world revolves around the dying and the rising of the Son.

The death and resurrection of Jesus is the event that all creation hopes for. When he found himself caught up in the first Easter, Cleopas began to re-imagine the entire Bible story. And so, as they walked together, Jesus began to unpack the Genesis story. What was true for Cleopas is true for us, too – or even more so. Having reflected on the good news of Easter, we can now view both the Bible and our world with a fresh perspective. So where to begin? Well, creation seems as good a place as any.

In the beginning

As Cleopas walked with Jesus on the road to Emmaus he had the privilege of hearing the one through whom creation was made expound creation's story. There can surely be no better way to discover the hope of the world. Think about it. In this conversation, Cleopas received a God's-eye view of creation. He heard what God was thinking about, and hoping for, when he made the universe. A more dynamic Bible study is hard to imagine.

Some years ago, I started a new job. The long list of responsibilities left me feeling somewhat overwhelmed. Desperately seeking peace, I finally consoled myself with this thought: 'If I can get through the first year without messing up too badly, I will probably get away with it.' I realize it's not the highest of ambitions, but it worked for me. I survived. That said, my sense of relief turned out to be short-lived. Mid-sigh, my bosses came to me with a whole new set of responsibilities and, with that, the same old worries and survival tactics returned. There was simply no time to sit back. It was back to go and start again. If only I could have had a few months, or even a few weeks, of stillness and respite. Now, I know I'm not alone. Anyone who has lived through a stressful time of transition knows how attractive stillness can look. The thought of existing in a permanent change-free zone with nothing on the horizon but more of the same, predictable comforts and homely routine, is strangely seductive. However, we all know that life is not like that. What's more, the Bible insists it was never meant to be like this.

Many think of the garden of Eden as a place of blissful changelessness. Here, man dwelt with God and God dwelt with man. Adam and Eve had it made. Our daily crises, pressuring expectations, pressing commitments and earnest efforts are a far cry from Eden. And yet while Eden was undoubtedly different, everything in the garden was not as still as we assume. For while in its first flush God's creation was pure and innocent, neither his work nor their work was necessarily complete. Put simply, God always hoped for more from creation.

Jesus' Bible study on creation was, in part, a dynamic event because creation itself is dynamic. In the beginning, while all was well with his world, God had a hope for creation. As they walked along the road, the rhythm of their feet reminded them that creation is on the go, it is heading in a certain direction. Here lies a common misconception about part of the creation story: God didn't rest on the Sabbath because his work was over, only to be woken a few days letter by the fall. God rested on the Sabbath because, having made the world, the work of creation was only just beginning. It is for this reason that the Bible's first book is called Genesis, the book of beginnings. Genesis was never meant to be a happy ending, only a happy beginning. In this way, the creation story represents the beginning of God's hope for his children, creatures and creation.

Parents everywhere speak of the unique hope that comes with the birth of a child. I can vividly remember the moment when, in the midst of a long and complex labour, the doctors informed us that our soon to be newborn son was in distress. Within seconds, my wife was rushed into the nearest operating theatre. As the nurse suited me up in a green gown with matching mask I was overcome by an irrational fear that I might be too tired to take the baby after the birth. Having not slept for the best part of two days, I was exhausted. Fearing the effects that sleep deprivation might have upon my fatherly debut, I quickly downed a handful of caffeine pills and a Diet Coke. I was ready!

In my naiveté, I had not taken into account the natural adrenalin kick which comes with the birth of your first child. Half an hour later, when Joe finally entered the world, I experienced – for the first and last time, I should add – the symptoms associated with mind-expanding drugs. The combination of a natural stimulant with a month's worth of caffeine resulted in a seriously heady cocktail. With camcorder in hand, I remember dancing around the paediatrician like Steven Spielberg on speed. How she ever examined Joe, I'll never know. My voice seemed two octaves higher and a thousand decibels louder. It was as if I was breathing helium and speaking through Iron Maiden's sound system. All of my senses were heightened. I was alive like never before or since.

In spite of the trauma that preceded his birth, Joe was perfect. And while part of me wishes I could have bottled that moment and held on to that elation and ecstasy, I didn't want Joe to remain in that state. I had hoped for a son, not for a baby. My hope was for a relationship. I wanted to share stories and adventures, prayers and possibilities. In fact, even while I was over the moon in the delivery room there was plenty about the baby phase that I was already looking forward to getting past – the dirty nappies, perpetual feeding, endless crying and yet more sleep deprivation, to name but a few of these things. For us as his parents, Joe's birth was not the sum of our hope, but simply the beginning.

God's hope for creation is as personal as that of any mother or father. In the creation of Adam and Eve, God expresses this hope for humankind. God's hope was not limited to his two firstborn in the garden – his hope extended to every human that will ever walk the face of the earth. He hopes for you and me. And his desire is not simply that we should exist. His hopes are dynamic. Adam and Eve are not the first human products on creation's conveyor belt. They are, rather, the first of God's children. And the Creator has high hopes for all of the children into whom he breathes his life – including you and me. He longs to nurture a relationship with us, watch us grow and develop and join with us in the adventure which he plans and purposes for creation.

Adam and Eve were not created to lead lives of changeless, eternal bliss in Eden. They were to care for the earth through all its changing seasons, to oversee the countless new species of creatures and plants and then, as if that were not a big enough job description, God gave them another command: 'Go forth and multiply' (Gen. 1:28). Adam and Eve were also to populate the earth – to fill the world with children and initiate many happy beginnings.

Time for creation

Jesus' big hopeful story began with creation – in fact, it began before creation. It started out with the hopes and dreams that God had before the beginning of time, through every millisecond of history and on to eternity. The size and scope of God's hope, as we keep discovering, continues to grow. For this reason, it cannot be revealed in a moment. God cannot take us to one side and explain to us all that we'll ever need to know. There is no potent hope serum that he can inject into us so that we might capture his eternal hope in one shot. He reveals his hopes in time as we walk along life's way. We are to hear, learn and experience his hopes in the passing moments of our everyday lives. We discover them as we read, pray, walk and talk. In the same way that it took time for the risen Jesus to reveal himself to Cleopas on the road to Emmaus, it takes time for us to understand God's hopes and plans for our lives, not to mention for the world at large. Finally, to understand the full dimensions of this hope we must be prepared to journey beyond our own time and space. We must explore God's hope throughout history.

The journey to Emmaus represents one of the first recorded attempts at time travel. As they walked, Jesus led Cleopas on a journey through time. He returned him to a time before time, when God decided to create the world. He led him through Hebrew history, retelling the stories of his ancestors. He reminded Cleopas of the lessons he learnt as a child and of his own teaching prior to the crucifixion. By outlining the biblical story so far, Jesus provided a step-by-step guide to God's hope for creation. The God of Israel and of the church is not the great Clockmaker in the Sky, an artisan who fashioned a world and then withdrew, allowing it to run its course without him. The dynamic God that we see in Jesus is one who has hopes and plans for the world he has made. He involves himself in creation, and hence the world is not a one-off invention but a long-term project.

In the same way that God's revelation takes time, so too does God's creation. That is, in part, the point of the resurrection. In rising from the dead Jesus proved that he is the Lord of all and the instigator of new creation. As we discovered in the last chapter, the resurrection marked the beginning of a new day, an era when resurrection is not simply hoped for but confirmed and assured. Through Jesus, the time of resurrection has come to pass for now and for ever. In this time, Jesus heralds God's work of new creation and calls us to prepare for a new heaven and earth. All of this requires one ingredient – an ingredient upon which all creation relies and yet that is hardly ever noticed. God's hopes and plans, creation and revelation all take time. It is the creation of *time* which makes life and history, jokes and stories, the past, present and future possible. In short, it is the making of time which enables God's hopes to be heard and fulfilled.

For as long as I can remember, I've enjoyed cooking. I'm not sure whether it's the opportunity to be creative, make a mess or consume the results that I love the most. However, I love to prepare food. None of this is to say that I'm any good at it. In fact, my culinary skills are often undone by one great weakness. As an aside, I would like to blame this flaw upon my mother. Like most mothers, my mother is armed with hundreds of couplets and clichés by which to navigate life's way. One of her favourites goes like this: 'Patience is a virtue, possess it if you can, often in a woman, rarely in a man.' Having heard my mum repeat this rhyme endlessly when I was a child, I suspect that I became impatient in a deliberate attempt to be more manly.

That said, my impatience has completely dashed my hopes of becoming a world-class chef. For while they work quickly, great chefs require endless patience. I'm never patient enough to prepare the ingredients ahead of time. I can never wait for the oven to reach the correct temperature. I am even too impatient to wait for the food to cook. I find myself, in a semi-crazed state, returning again and again to sneak a peek. Unwilling to inspect the food through dim glass and in dusky light, I open the oven repeatedly for a closer look. Proficient cooks among you will know that this habit can, in culinary terms, prove fatal. Every time one opens the oven the temperature drops, thereby arresting the cooking process, prolonging the time and diminishing the overall results. Despite the curse which my mother repeatedly spoke over me as a child, I hope one day to learn patience. But I don't want patience simply so as to improve my cooking. I want patience because it takes time to come to terms with God's hope for the world.

Why are we so slow to think of time as part of God's creation? Is it purely a result of the fast-paced instamatic-madness of the modern world? While this is undoubtedly part of the problem, a larger challenge lurks nearby. We don't think about time because time is hard to think about. If you don't agree, then just try thinking about anything without it. While we can visualize a world without certain objects or things, spaces or places, it is much harder to conceive of a timeless reality. On one hand, it is possible to imagine a world without spiders, pot plants or mountains. On the other, it is practically impossible to imagine a world without days, weeks, months or time. For as any decent daydreamer knows, it takes time to imagine things in the first place.

Like good food, good conversation and everything else that is good in life, good stories take time. The story with which the Bible begins is a perfect example. The creation of time can be seen in three essential aspects of the Genesis narrative. First, the creation story is ordered into six separate days; as we have said, it takes time to make a world (Gen. 1:3–31). Second, the Creator begins by making light to distinguish different times of day and night (Gen. 1:3–5). Third – and this point is easily missed – time is intrinsic to the story's genre. Genesis chapter one takes the form of a poem. Poetry is a form of writing and narration which makes special use of time. Poets order their words into rhymes and rhythms, thus making a feature of the temporal process. Put simply, poetry plays with time through language. We conclude, therefore, that the creation story makes much of the role of time in God's creation.

From the very beginning, time has been part of God's plan for this world. If the world was supposed to be static, just another object to sit on God's heavenly mantelpiece, there would be no need for time. What's more, there would be no future to hope for. However, from the beginning creation has been moving through time. In time, God is taking creation somewhere. Even more importantly, in creation God is making time for us. This statement is hugely encouraging. In creation, God chose to make time and space for you and me so that we might know him in our time and form part of his hope for all eternity.

By underlining the importance of time within God's creation, the poetry of Genesis chapter one helps us to grasp the timely hope of God in creation. It may seem as though we have a long way to go before his hopes are finally fulfilled, but the important thing is that God has made all the time in the world available for this journey. Of all the ways in which God works to perform his wonders, the medium of time must be one of the most mysterious and magnificent. In the same way that we cannot imagine a world without time, there is simply nothing that God cannot do in time.

As a kid I never understood the phrase 'Time is the greatest healer.' Surely healing is dramatic and instantaneous. If it takes 'time', how can that be a healing? Isn't that just recovery, a case of slowly getting better? However, the older I get, the more I understand it. Along with the rest of creation, time has its uses. In fact, you might say that time is particularly useful to God. After all, it is hard to think of anything that can be done without it. Hence, God makes time for a purpose. In the same way that he has plans for the planet and his people, he also has plans for time. If there are certain things that God chooses to do through individuals, communities or parts of his creation, there must be some things that he chooses to do through time. Some of us are forced to learn this lesson the hard way.

Those of us who expect instantaneous answers to every prayer soon learn that God simply doesn't work that way. Unfortunately, the world is littered with disillusioned Christians who interpreted the gap between prayer and response as a sign of God's displeasure or, worse still, his non-existence. While we might want God to bypass the temporal process and teleport us to the moment of revelation and release, creation, it appears, is not often set up in this way. But far from proving God's absence, the passing of time is always evidence of the God who makes time for his creation. Our journey through time is just one of the ways in which God fulfils the hopes that he has for us.

I once heard a preacher tell the story of how he found himself speaking at a conference with one of his heroes. Having been introduced to this man, he was eager to impress.

'So, where are you travelling to next?' he asked this international speaker.

'I'm taking a seven-day silent retreat at a local monastery,' he replied.

Wishing to sustain the conversation, he eagerly threw out his next question. 'So what will you get out of that?' he asked. As soon as he heard his own words he wished that he had rehearsed them in his own head first.

His hero looked at him with great humility and some pity and replied, 'You know, I really don't know. I figure God just likes it when I show up.'

We could all do with learning how to show up for God on a more regular basis. But we need to remember that, regardless of how good we are at showing up for him, the Creator of time shows up for us on a minute-by-minute basis. As Cleopas could testify, whether we recognize him or not

Jesus does walk with us. In the same way that Jesus accompanied his friend to Emmaus, so Jesus joins us along our way – whether we're heading somewhere important or to a little nowhere town down the road. As a result, our lives are but one prolonged conversation on a long and dusty road. At times the road is easy, at others it is hard. Sometimes we find words easily and sometimes not. Occasionally we gain glimpses of God; occasionally it's as though he's dead, buried and nowhere to be seen. But in each and every moment Jesus joins us by the power of his Spirit and makes his Father's hope present.

The remarkable part of this story on the road to Emmaus is not the time that Cleopas spent with Jesus. After all, for most of the journey he didn't even know it was Jesus. What is truly remarkable is that the resurrected Jesus took the time to be with Cleopas. Having made time for us, God longs to enjoy our journey with us. And while impatient people like me seem never to have enough time for anyone or anything, God always has time for us. In fact, he has all the time in the world. As Cleopas discovered along the way, God's single greatest hope – the hope that creation would recognize who he is and come to worship him – also takes time. It took Cleopas a long time to come to terms with God's revelation in Jesus. It took a lifetime of faith and practice, the years he spent with Jesus, the hours that it took to walk to Emmaus and the time necessary to prepare a decent meal.

Perfecting hope

One wonders what kind of consolation this stranger's exposition of Genesis provided for Cleopas and his companion, stricken with grief as they were and possibly fearing for their safety. Was this tale of a time before death in the garden of Eden meant to distract them from their present burdens? No, it was not. The Genesis story is not a historical drama with nudity and fig leaves. As we have seen, the creation story is God's first expression of hope for his world. By telling the story of the planet's past Jesus reminded his companions of creation's future. The story of creation is not only a lesson in history but also a prophecy of God's hope for humanity. The Genesis story speaks as much about our destination as it does of our origins. It is a signpost to the future as well as a memorial of the past. This story reminds us what creation was and what it will one day be.

Chapter one of Genesis describes creation bursting with God's goodness. Once again, the point is in the poetry. Following each individual creative act, God surveyed his work to see 'that it was good' (Gen. 1:3–31). He speaks his highest praise of the whole of creation following the birth of humankind. 'God saw all that he had made, and it was very good' (Gen. 1:31). Not once in these verses does the text refer to creation as perfect. For this reason theologians often state that God made the world to be good, but not perfect. The Hebrew word for 'good', which occurs repeatedly in Genesis 1, is tov, which has the sense of 'pleasing'. By describing the world as good, Genesis is not suggesting that God did a bad job of creation – far from it. Rather, the poet invites us to view the original world as pure, innocent, unblemished, holy and pleasing to its maker. This world in Genesis 1 is good but ultimately incomplete.

To apply the argument, one illustration should suffice. In the garden, where all was good but not perfect, it was possible for Adam and Eve to sin and die. Neither of these outcomes was necessary, but both were possible. Tragically, as we know, Adam and Eve fell, sullied the goodness of creation and faced the consequences of their own mortality as a result (Gen. 3). The story of Adam and Eve points to a world where sin and death are possible, a world which is good but not perfect. So what would it take to make a perfect world?

The Hebrew word for 'perfect' is *tam*. The root verb of this word can be translated 'to be completed'. Hence the biblical word for perfection does not simply render something pure and innocent. Rather, perfection also entails fulfilment and completion. In biblical terms, to say that something is perfect is to say that it has been completed. As a result, it is impossible for the world to be perfect in the first chapter of Genesis. After all, this poem marks the beginning of the creation story, not the end. In short, while it's off to a good start, the world is some way from being completed or perfected. Returning to our illustration, we see that at the point when God perfects creation, death and sin will no longer be possible. No one will sin or die in the new creation, for by then Jesus' death will have defeated all sin and his resurrection will have done away with all death. In this perfected creation, humanity will experience the eternal possibilities of human freedom without the devastating effects of sin.

Used carefully, these two small words, *tov* and *tam*, frame the entire story of creation. In the beginning God created a world that is good and, in time, he hopes to complete creation and perfect the job that he started. Once again we arrive at the dynamic mobility of creation. The world was made to be something and yet become so much more. When I was eighteen, my Dad bought me my first car. It was only a second-hand Ford Fiesta but to me it was very good. After all, it did everything I wanted it to do. It got me from A to B and gave me freedom. In the years that I owned the car, I made numerous improvements to the vehicle. I replaced the radio with a CD player, bought new seats and a stuck a go-faster stripe down the sides. Unfortunately, my plans to perfect the car by turning it into something more resembling a Ferrari than a Fiesta came to an abrupt stop when I crashed it twice on one day. However, given a few more years my project would have surely been completed.

From the beginning of time God had high hopes for creation. His plan was to take that which was innocent and good and transform it into something that was complete and perfect. By declaring that the world was good and pleasing to God, the author of Genesis informs us that the world was fit for God's purpose. Having finished the first part of the job, God saw that everything necessary to bring about his full, final and perfect hope for creation was in place. How did he intend to pull off such a grand plan? He planned to use humankind. God created us to be his partners in this project to complete and perfect creation. From the start, God planned for us to be ambassadors of hope. But can we really deliver on these expectations? Is it realistic for God to use us to improve upon the goodness of his creation?

Michelangelo was one of the greatest sculptors of his day, and one of his finest works is entitled the Pietà. Standing near the entrance of St Peter's in the Vatican, this colossal work depicts the lifeless Christ being held by his mother following his removal from the cross. When the French cardinal Jean de Billheres commissioned Michelangelo to create the work, Michelangelo sent his assistants to scour many quarries in search of the best marble. Given the importance of the work and the reputation of the artist, only an exceptional piece would do. Having acquired the marble, a rock formed by God himself, Michelangelo began to cut, chisel, polish and shine the rock into the image of Jesus and his mother. Inspired by God, Michelangelo took two years to transform this raw material into the most powerful depiction of God's perfect Son.

By taking him back to the beginning of time, Jesus was reminding Cleopas that Genesis was only the beginning. While it was certainly a very good beginning, it was only the start of the Creator's hopes for creation. By taking Cleopas to the furthest reaches of the past Jesus reminded him that God had not finished yet. All of us who despair about the present state of things can take hope. The present state of things is not the result of God's inability to make the world good but rather a sign that he has much unfinished business. As we look to the future, we can be sure that he has a plan to perfect creation. What's more, we ourselves are part of this plan. As the travellers drew closer to Emmaus, Cleopas was about to discover that God's hope for the world was very much alive. What's more, he would soon discover that he had an essential role to play in the realization of God's hope for the world.

Hope for the fallen

Talk of creation's original goodness and God's perfecting plan is all very well, but how hopeful is it given Cleopas' present situation? Lest we forget, at this point in the journey Cleopas' hope of resurrection had yet to be vindicated. Could he really believe in creation's current goodness and future perfection when he'd just seen his friend hung out to die? We do need to ask this question. After all, the previous weekend's events formed a convincing case for creation's ultimate hopelessness and the irretrievably fallen nature of humankind. From where Cleopas stood, the consoling message that 'God had a plan' and 'these things take time' must have been cold comfort. To his mind, the crucifixion must have seemed like the one event which could destroy God's hope for creation once and for all. The situation in which Cleopas finds himself is a million miles from the goodness of Eden or the perfection of the planet. Two thousand years later, the question still remains. In a world which can sometimes resemble hell more than it does heaven, what hope does God have left?

A few years back I found myself in desperate need of a holiday. Having looked forward to two weeks of sunbathing and sleeping, reading and eating, we finally arrived at our hotel. My expectations of our time away were reorganized in the first hour. After all, having two young kids rendered my aspirations totally unrealistic. Having checked in, our whole family marched straight towards the pool. We were armed and ready with towels, swimming costumes and buckets of factor five thousand sunscreen. I led the procession, it being my job to scout for vacant sunbeds. I turned around to check the progress of the troops and couldn't help but notice that Joe was sprinting towards the pool. When he reached the edge of the water he took a flying leap. At this point, it dawned on me that Joe couldn't swim. For a second, time stood still. Joe was suspended in mid-air above the pool. Unfortunately this didn't last. As real time resumed, Joe crashed into the water and sunk like a stone to the bottom. Standing fully clothed by the side of the pool, I began to wonder whether I should remove my shoes before jumping in. My deliberation was violently interrupted by the quicker part of my brain shouting, 'No, you idiot! Jump in and save him before he drowns!' Headlong and forthwith, I hurled myself into the pool and pulled Joe out.

Thinking back, it's my relative slowness to act that surprises me. You see, I had already figured that at some point in the fortnight ahead I might need to rescue him from just such a perilous situation. After all, Joe was a four-year-old boy and this is precisely the kind of thing that four-year-olds do. What I hadn't expected was that this would happen within our first hour. Reflecting further has caused me to reflect on God's foresight in creation. After all, an all-knowing God must have known that we would fall. Did he always know that he'd have to jump in and save us? Is he surprised by our fall from grace? And if so, how long did it take for him to make up his mind about whether to pull us out or leave us to drown? Well, if God is omniscient – as classical theology insists – then none of this could have surprised him.

One question that has haunted theologians over the centuries concerns God's foreknowledge. If God is omniscient (all-knowing), then he surely must have foreseen the fall. But if he knew that this would happen, why did God create the world in the first place? Wouldn't it have been better not to create the world at all than to watch it destroyed by sin? Many theologians have defended God's all-knowing nature with a powerful proviso. Not only did God know that humankind would fall before creation, but he also knew what it would take to turn things around. In short, God knew that creation would prove costly. As Karl Barth, the greatest theologian of the twentieth century, has argued, in creation God made two decisions at the same time: one to make the world and another to save it.

From the start, God knew that we'd run and jump and drown in sin. And from the start he knew that his Son would have to give his own life to save us. With this, two subsequent revelations come to light. First, the fall didn't surprise the Almighty. He did not look at a sorry Adam and Eve and declare, 'Whoops, I didn't think that would happen.' Second, the commitment to create the world was, at one and the same time, a decision to give his only Son to save creation. From before the beginning of time Jesus was the hope of the world. For him and through him all things were made. In him and by him the world will be saved. As Cleopas walked down the road to Emmaus, he was clueless that the very hope and saviour of creation had joined him.

A friend of mine has recently opened a number of Christian high schools. The initiative has been a subject of controversy in the secular media. In one interview, Steve was asked whether the schools' biology teachers would teach Genesis chapter one to their pupils. 'Not just the biology teachers,' he cried. 'All of our teachers are going to teach Genesis chapter one. In fact, we're going to teach Genesis chapter one every day, in every lesson, to every student and then to every parent, visitor and member of staff.' As smoke rose from the hack's notepad Steve went on, 'And the reason we're going to teach Genesis chapter one is this: Because above all else, Genesis says that God made the world and thinks it's good. What's more, he made you and he thinks you're good.' The pen came to an abrupt halt. The journalist looked stunned. After all, it's not every day that a Fleet Street journalist is described as 'good'.

Imagine for a moment what would happen if Steve's message got out to every individual on the planet. What difference would this make to our communities, the nations and the world? Furthermore, when God says humans are good, he doesn't just mean that they're worth saving when they fall. As God says about creation in Genesis 1, he means that they can be used for good, that they're fit for his purposes. Put simply, human beings can be trusted to bring about God's original and ultimate hopes for creation. It may be hard to believe news this good, but that is the overriding theme of the creation-salvation story. And there is not a single person in the history of the world upon whom God does not look in this way. As G.K. Chesterton wrote in *Father Brown*, 'All men matter. You matter, I matter. It's the hardest thing to believe . . . We matter to God. God only knows why.' This is surely one of the most surprising twists in the whole of the Bible story.

As he shared a meal with the risen Jesus later that evening, Cleopas tasted the first fruit of the new creation. Here, Luke draws a powerful parallel between the events in Emmaus and the creation story. The moment at which Cleopas and his companion's eyes were opened (Lk. 24:31) is a direct reference to Adam and Eve first noticing their nakedness after the fall (Gen. 3:7). However, the effect of Cleopas' eye-opening experience could not have been more different. While Adam and Eve were confronted with the reality of sin and the fall of creation, Cleopas was presented with the dawn of new creation. Sitting before him was the second Adam, the living proof that God had entrusted human beings with his hope for the restoration of his creation. As a result, humanity had no longer to be defined by the moral frailty and physical vulnerability of Adam and Eve. Instead we can attach our identity to Jesus, the one who conquered sin on our behalf. Suddenly, the evidence that God will conquer sin, destroy death and complete creation was there for

Cleopas to see. Jesus' presence was a signpost to this perfect future tense.

As I mentioned earlier, it took me a while to understand how time might heal. However, I now understand that the time which God has made for his creation and his people is enough – not only to heal the world, but also to perfect it. God alone knows exactly how much time it will take for the world to recognize, worship and work for him. However, the time has already come for Cleopas and all disciples of the risen Jesus everywhere to glimpse the world to come and work towards creation's completion. One sermon I heard in my youth featured a quote that has stuck with me all these years. I'm not sure I understood it completely at the time, but it resonated deep within me. Unfortunately it hasn't become one of those oft-repeated maxims, but I think it should. It is the natural epilogue to our discussion of time as the greatest healer: 'God's healing is only ever complete in the new heaven and the new earth.' In this world, things won't only get better, they'll be perfect. It's only a matter of time.

4

Hope in the Desert

The road ahead

On the road to Emmaus Jesus explained the whole of salvation history, beginning with God's good creation in Genesis 1. Having explored how this creation will one day be restored to perfection, in this chapter we will consider the crucial role of the exodus – in Israel's history and our own. To understand the exodus story is to understand what it is to be part of God's people.

As we chart this next stage on the journey to Emmaus we will explore the role that stories play in all of our lives. As they did for Cleopas and his countrymen, stories and testimonies form an essential part of our personal and communal identities. However, the story of the exodus is not simply about one nation's journey towards self-awareness and fulfilment. In Exodus, Israel believes that she has uncovered God's story; in these tales we discover the character and nature of the one who made the heavens and the earth. Hence Exodus is as much God's story as it is Israel's.

The story of Israel's exodus from Egypt reveals the character and nature of the one who made the heavens and the earth. Just as God called Israel to become part of his story through the exodus, so Christ extends that invitation to everyone. In this chapter we'll explore what it looks like to accept this invitation and deepen our knowledge of, and involvement in, God's story. We'll see that the story of the exodus anticipates the future of God's people as much as it reminds them of God's mighty working in the past.

The adventures of Moses and Israel in Exodus provided Cleopas with the possibility of hopeful living. But as Cleopas and his companions saw, and as we shall see for ourselves in this chapter, it is ultimately in the life, death and resurrection of Jesus that a whole new chapter in the story of God and his people begins.

> And beginning with Moses and all the Prophets, he explained to them what was said in all the Scriptures concerning himself (Lk. 24:27).

The old ones are the best ones

As he explained the Easter events, Jesus continued his walk through the Old Testament. Having rehearsed the story of Genesis, a book which Moses was credited with writing, Jesus turned to Exodus, Moses' own biography. For a Jew, God's hope was inseparable from the exodus story. In fact, some rabbis thought that Exodus should be taught prior to Genesis, such was its importance. God's highest hopes for creation concerned his people. Above all, he wanted a people to call his own. Having decided to create people, God needed somewhere to put them. Creation became the divine solution to this problem. In Exodus, we read of the calling and forming of God's people. Therefore, where God's hopes are concerned, Exodus is the main feature, with Genesis as its prequel.

The book of Exodus is not only Moses' life story; it is also the key to Israel's national identity, the pattern for Jesus' own life and ministry and an essential guide for the church on what it means to be God's people. It's hardly surprising, then, that this story has been told so often.

At times the life of a preacher can be tough. Admittedly it's rarely as difficult as we make it sound – particularly we who moan endlessly about the pressures of travel, the pain of going to interesting places, suffering care from the kindest people on the planet and the trials of time spent in airport lounges (although this last one can really be a pain). However, although it may not be the most arduous of jobs, it is also not without its pressures – one of the most persistent and pressing of these being the quest for new stories. While the Bible provides us with endless theological material, there are only so many great stories with which to illustrate this. As a result, many of us have hard drives filled with sermons but can fit all of our stories onto a couple of pages. One of the problems is that while congregations quickly forget scriptural insights, they always remember the stories.

While most can tell a story, certain preachers have the added spiritual gift of 'story-making'. Used well, this gift can propel a speaker into the premier league. If one is gifted in this narrative art, daily incidents in the preacher's life will, once 'storyfied', translate perfectly into almost any talk or sermon. Whether it's introducing their taxi driver to Jesus, bumping into Nelson Mandela at the cash point or narrowly averting a plane crash, for these guys every day brings a new story. Those of us without the gift live lives of quiet envy. Impoverished, we make do by squeezing the same old stories into every talk. We then pray hard that those who heard us last week will get stuck in traffic next week. Incidentally, it is for this reason that itinerant preaching is so beloved. When we speak to different audiences, all of our stories are new stories.

As it is, so it was in the beginning and ever more shall be. Despite the volumes of wisdom, law and inspiration contained within the Old Testament, it's the stories that we most remember and come back to. In fact, it's fair to say that the genius of Scripture rests in the story. God's revelation is not limited to a bunch of rules, sayings or principles. The Bible is one big fat book of stories, great and small. Although Israel's history books have many tales to tell, the story of Exodus stands out. This one tale holds the key to her past, present and future. In whatever era, predicament or nation she finds herself, this story is always prophetic and ever hopeful. To this day, while scattered throughout the world and divided into many different sects, traditions and cultures, Jewish people find their identity in this one story about their ancestors and their great hero, Moses.

Israel was cooped up under Egyptian rule and forced to work as builders for Pharaoh, and Exodus records her miraculous escape. Having failed to secure his people's release through diplomatic channels, their intrepid leader Moses prayed for another way out. Israel followed God's instructions and hosted a huge party, called Passover. God then proceeded to set his people free. In the hours that followed, a whole nation arose and walked across the Red Sea. Having made a way through the sea for his people, God allowed the waters to crash over Pharaoh's armies as they gave chase. Over the decades that followed, Moses led his people towards their new home – a holy land flowing with milk and honey. And over the course of this journey, a bunch of builders were built into God's chosen nation. The story can still seem strange, almost surreal, and yet billions of people around the world would not exist without it.

What were Cleopas and his companion thinking about their fellow traveller? Were they disconcerted by his interest in Jesus' death and supposed resurrection? Or were they shocked that he seemed to be the only one in all Jerusalem who was oblivious to the events of the previous days? Were they uneasy as he quizzed them and pressed them to share disturbing scenes and difficult details? Or were they blown away by his intuitive insights into creation and their present situation? Where the creation story helped the Jews to understand the world in which they found themselves, Exodus helped them to understand their identity as a people. Here is a story they had heard and told a thousand times. No matter how uncertain their present situation, in this tale they could find solace and security. If any story could turn hopelessness and pain into hope and possibility, it was this one.

I'm gonna' tell you a story

What was it about the exodus story that provided such solace for Cleopas and his countrymen? After all, trying to soothe their worried brows by reminding them of their ancestors' good old days seems less than comforting and more akin to showing someone with money worries a Discovery Channel documentary about the history of banking. So what is it about this story?

In his star-studded career, Steven Spielberg has told many stories. Yet this Jewish film-maker seems destined always to return to one story in particular. And yes, you guessed it – it's the story of the exodus. In *Schindler's List*, Spielberg projects Oskar Schindler as a Moses-type figure leading many Jews to safety during the Holocaust. In the film, Schindler's gravestone is inscribed with a verse from the Talmud: 'He who saves a single life saves the world entire.' *Saving Private Ryan*, another Spielberg film about World War II, explores a similar theme as a band of soldiers liberates a colleague trapped behind enemy lines. And in *The Prince of Egypt*, Spielberg goes all the way and puts the exodus story on to the big screen. But why does he return to this tale so regularly?

The story of the exodus provides Israel with the key to their identity. For Spielberg, as for all who came after Moses, telling the exodus story is like breathing. For as long as she lives, Israel will remember and retell this story. We only have to look at Jesus to verify this. At the Last Supper, only hours before his execution, he took time to celebrate Passover. For his last meal, Jesus chose to re-enact the exodus story once more. In his darkest days, this meal symbolized his hope. A few days later, as he walked with Cleopas to Emmaus, he told the story once more. Why? Because like Steven Spielberg, every one of us discovers who we are by hearing and telling stories. Put simply, to be human is to enjoy a good story. Whether it's about our first kiss, most embarrassing moment, proudest achievement or hope for the future, stories help us to find our place in the world. It's not surprising, then, that God uses stories to bring us new hope. For when we try to understand who we are as God's people we inevitably come back to our story as his creatures and his story as our Creator. In fact, as history teaches us, any attempt to understand our lives without attention to the importance of story is bound for failure.

In the seventeenth century the philosopher René Descartes sought to prove God's existence. If he could first prove creation's existence, he reasoned, then surely the Creator's reality would be a philosophical formality. To prove creation, or so his logic ran, he simply needed to prove that he himself was real. If he could prove that he was part of creation, then he could confirm the presence of God the Creator. He locked himself away and declared that he would not be seen again until he could philosophically prove his own existence. After what seemed like an age, he sprang forth and declared: 'I think, therefore I am!' We know with the wisdom of hindsight that he ran ahead of himself, and philosophers have worked tirelessly ever since to refute his theory. Although I'm not aware of anyone having denied Descartes' outright existence, few believe that his 'proof' adequately confirmed it.

Descartes' attempt to prove our connection with creation and the Creator by reason alone provided a less than satisfactory understanding of what it means to be human. In fact, when we approach human beings this way they seem to become less than human. While human beings have been gifted with amazing mental powers, we are also more than the sum of our thoughts. For starters, we have bodies as well as brains. So is the secret to being human more about the body than the brain?

In 2002, the German doctor Gunther von Hagens acquired some notoriety by being the first to perform an autopsy in front of a live TV audience. The millions who watched in the discomfort of their own homes saw a brutal process in which a dead body was clinically deconstructed into its constituent parts. By the end, the body had been stripped bare and relocated on, and in, various benches, jars, bottles and containers. For those who had never seen our anatomy in such detail, and who could stomach the sight of it, the programme was educational. However, the process of dissecting a body in this way only served to destroy what little was left of this human form.

Attempts to limit humanity to our ability to reason or to a series of bodily parts are doomed to failure. Humans are much more than the sum of their mental and biological capacities. So where do we discover what it means to be human? The answer lies in our story. To paraphrase Descartes, we might say, 'I have a story, therefore I am.' I have a past and a present. I was born in this place, grew up there, live here and would one day like to go there. I fell in love with a girl. We got married and had kids. I went to school, to university, to work. I had a life-changing experience last week. I'm going to move to another community next year. And so on.

We understand who we are by way of our story. We chart our understanding of the world and of the Creator through anecdotes and memories, books and teaching, parables and personal experience. Put together, these form our testimony – the story of how faith has impacted and directs our life. These stories are never entitled 'Me, Myself and I'. For we always share our story with others. Our story is, in part, their story – and vice versa. To be human is to live one story among many stories, or to share our story with many others. Either way, the basic statements that we make about ourselves reveal something of our story. Our stories hold the secret of our humanity. They help us to understand the world and provide us with hope. If we take away our stories, we are nothing but a brain and bodily parts. On the other hand, if we seek to connect our stories with those of others, we discover that our lives are part of something much bigger. We realize that our story is part of one gigantic overarching story – the story from creation to redemption penned by the Creator.

The disciples also understood their identity through a series of stories. As Israelites, their story was part of a national history. The exodus story provided personal hope and consolation because it was their communal story, their family history, the story of who they were as *God's* people. As such, it helped them to know who they were, where they came from and where they might be going.

The story that began in Egypt those millennia ago continues in our time and place. In the person of the risen Christ, God guides our journeys from captivity to liberation, from desert wanderings to glorious homecomings. As did Cleopas, and all Israel, we too will reach our destination. Having arrived, we will look back on our stories with holy perspective and see how God's goodness prevailed in every detail of our lives. On the road to Emmaus, Cleopas was about to make a similar discovery – every step he took brought him closer to the next and final chapter in God's story.

Whose story is it anyway?

By telling him the story of the exodus Jesus reminded Cleopas not only of his personal life story, but also of his place in *the* story. Israel, Judaism, the Old Testament, Jesus and the church – they all depend on the exodus. But even above and beyond all that, the exodus story is first and foremost a lesson in theology. It is not just the historical event but the theological content of Exodus which provides hope for God's people. Put simply, Exodus is as much about God as it is about Israel.

Pete, a friend of mine, told me the story of being invited to lunch by a new colleague. He arrived at the imposing office block and was shown straight to the top floor. In his colleague's cavernous office he sat down with his host at the oak dining table in the middle of the room. Moments later, a waiter wheeled a trolley of the finest foods along-side the table and then, without a word, turned and left the room. Thinking it was self-service, Pete rose to help himself. 'Do sit down,' his host asked politely, 'I would like to serve you.' Now the story is truly unremarkable, which is more than can be said for the man who served the lunch. As the leader of a huge global organization, he could quite easily have asked the waiter to stay or even fired him for not finishing the job. He could have also allowed his much more junior colleague to dish up. And yet he did neither. From the beginning he had decided to serve, a decision which said more about his leadership than any résumé ever could.

Exodus is a truly remarkable story. The most remarkable thing about it is not the plot itself but the main character. And by that I don't mean Moses, or even the people. For while Exodus tells us much about Moses' leadership and about the Israelite's escape from Egypt, survival in the wilderness and conquest of the promised land, the real star of the show is God himself. The exodus story preserves a remarkable record of God's faithful interest, miraculous power and persistent hope. Through Israel's adventures, we glimpse the Creator and Redeemer of the universe. As God orchestrates their miraculous escape from Egypt, protects and provides for them in the wilderness, reveals his law and brings them into the promised land, Israel discovers who God is. By retelling this tale, Israel celebrates the fact that God's story and her story have become one and the same.

A few years ago I completed a prolonged period of study. Towards the end of this time, I shared a coffee with Brian. Brian had been my tutor when I started to study theology but had since retired – an event which may have been brought on prematurely due to the stress of teaching students like me. Brian, one of the kindest and cleverest people I know, has the habit of asking the most unobtrusive and yet intensely searching questions. 'So,' he began, 'how has study changed your life?' I proceeded to share enthusiastically how the course had extended my theological vocabulary, deepened my knowledge of Scripture, furthered my understanding of the tradition and so on. While the words continued to pour out, deep down I knew that the most obvious difference could be explained in three words. As I spewed forth addendum after addendum, this one simple phrase was playing over and over in my mind. I'm ashamed to say that I never did own up. All that education, and I hadn't the courage to muster three little words.

'I cry more.' There it is, confessed and off my chest. That's what I should have said, but I didn't have the guts. It's not that study made me more wobbly or less robust. I wasn't particularly touchy-feely when I started and I'm not that way now either. The difference is this: I now find myself regularly moved by the sheer truth, beauty and goodness of God.

Like Cleopas' meeting with the resurrected Jesus on the Emmaus road, God often takes me by surprise. Without warning, remembrances of the Bible story take my breath away. Aspects of God's character creep up and grab me. The contents of a book or lecture sometimes hit home suddenly. It happens when I try to sing certain songs, tell certain stories or pray certain prayers. It's not that I didn't know God before, but in these last few years, by his grace, I have a deepened understanding. The frequency of these poignancies increases at Christmas time. In the annual nightmare on the High Street, I'll often find myself suddenly and pleasantly mugged by a Christmas carol playing in the background. All it takes is one line. One simple and ancient lyric of how, at Christmas, God's story unfolded in Jesus. You see, it's not the recognition of acquired knowledge that moves me. It's the realization that God has joined us on the road. It's the conscious awareness that, in Jesus, God chose to write his story into our story. For this reason, I cry more. At this point, I can't help but think of these powerful lines from a well-known Christmas carol.

> How silently, how silently, the wondrous Gift is giv'n;
> So God imparts to human hearts the blessings of His
> Heav'n.
> No ear may hear His coming, but in this world of sin,
> Where meek souls will receive Him still, the dear Christ
> enters in.
>
> *'O Little Town of Bethlehem', Phillips Brooks (1835–93)*

I would give every line I have written, every sermon preached, to compose five lines as beautiful and revelatory as these. Here, Phillips Brooks captures one of the most profound points of all Christian theology. In fact, it is not too much to say that without this truth there would be no such thing as Christian theology. For while the decision that Christians make to give their lives to Jesus is remarkable, it is only an option at all because God gave himself first. Without God's liberating power, Israel would have remained in Egypt making bricks for Pharaoh. Had it not been for God's willingness to enter darkness, we could never bask in the light of the world. In the exodus, Israel became God's story in creation. At Christmas we celebrate a new chapter, in which God invites all humankind to hear and become part of his story. Jesus *is* God's story, for he is fully God. When we give our lives to Jesus, therefore, we become one with him and commit to re-enact his story in our story. At Passover, at Christmas, through the stories of Israel, in Jesus, in our day-to-day lives, God invites us to become part of his big story. As we discovered first in Jesus, then in creation and now in the exodus, we can find real hope only in this story.

One of the regular challenges that Christians face is our own ignorance of God's story. This failing can be the result of many different factors – uninspiring sermons, a lack of resources, a fear of study, leaders who discourage difficult questions and so forth. Whatever the reason for our lack of understanding and knowledge, the fact of the matter is that an ignorance of God's story leads to a serious deficit of hope. Recently, having challenged a congregation about this, I found myself on the receiving end of some serious complaints. I can sum up the gist of these concerns in one question: 'We want to know the Bible better, but where do we start?' One lady went so far as to tell me how her vicar had suggested reading the Bible in a year. It sounded like a good idea at the time until she nearly lost her faith somewhere in Leviticus. We could go on for some time assigning blame for why Christians struggle with God's story, but the constructive question is this: If it is an essential ingredient in learning to live hopefully, how can we deepen our understanding of God's story?

I would like to suggest four time-honoured ways for accomplishing this. First, we should make use of each other. For many, private study has become the dead end of their biblical knowledge. For some reason, the thought of locking themselves away by candlelight to study every name in

Chronicles is an instant turn-off to some people. For those of us who feel guilty about such incapacity, there is good news coming.

The concept of solitary Bible study was foreign to Cleopas and the disciples. They simply didn't have enough copies of the Scriptures to make this possible. From the beginning, learning God's story was a communal activity. Getting to grips with the Law, the Prophets and the Historical Books involved teamwork, games, exercises and rewards. People were taught not simply to learn it by themselves, but rather to perform it for one another. They sat together and discussed God's story. They argued about it, questioned it, acted it and shared it. We would do well to learn this lesson. If we wish to go deeper, we should begin by making use of the community that is God's people, the church. We should identify individuals and groups with whom we can gather and make God's story come to life. And we should remember that when we gather together, Jesus joins us: 'For where two or three come together in my name, there am I with them' (Mt. 18:20).

Second, we should make use of wise counsel. Why, we might ask, did Jesus take such an inordinate amount of time to teach Cleopas and his disciples? He invested this time because he was calling and equipping them to teach and share the truth with others. All of us know people who we love to talk to and learn from. We should take time to interact with these learned individuals, ask for their advice on books to read, raise questions and problems that we find along the way and ask for their help as we seek to go deeper.

Third, we should make use of good resources. While sometimes difficult to find, there are great resources available to

Christians who wish to enhance their understanding of the Bible and grasp of theology. Ask your local Bible college or university for a prospectus; investigate other training organizations and the programmes they offer; make use of books and small group materials recommended by your pastor or your local Christian bookshop; try something new and take a walk in a different part of the Christian tradition; sign up for a conference or a retreat; download podcast sermons from church and Christian radio websites. If your local congregation does not have a lending library of resources, you could start one.

Fourth, we can go deeper into the story by eating. In all seriousness, food has long been an essential ingredient for God's people as they search for hope. As children, Cleopas and his friends would have been rewarded with sweet treats as they developed their understanding. Through their lives they would have attended many family meals and national feasts, all staged to draw them deeper into God's story. This tradition goes back to the first Passover, the celebration which triggered their ancestors' escape from captivity. The Passover confirms that sharing food is an intrinsic part of the life of God's people. In eating together we share our lives, remember what God has done, are nourished by his life and find hope for the future. In short, the dinner table is the perfect place for us to experience God's community, and to share wise counsel and teaching.

A few years ago, my local church started a small group called 'Credo' (believe). Every Wednesday evening for a couple of months, the same group of six or so members gathered to share a meal and discuss God's story. Each week we met, having read the same chapter or article, and shared thoughts and questions. Most weeks those who gathered, most of whom had grown up in church, poured out questions that they'd always wanted to ask but were too afraid. Together we explored the problem questions and the possible answers. Often we went home with more to think about and always we discovered new aspects of God's story

By reminding him of the exodus, Jesus reassured Cleopas that the hope of the world rests in the story of God and his people. What Cleopas did not yet know was how important his role would be in the very next chapter of that story.

Back to the future

By retelling the exodus story Jesus also affirmed Cleopas' identity as one of God's children and reminded him that God is present in his story. No matter how difficult the past few days had been, he explained, God's promises continued to hold true. God doesn't excuse himself when life gets tough; as good as his word, God joins us on the road and sticks with us, no matter how rocky it becomes. This reminder of the exodus set Cleopas' sights on the big picture – past events, current affairs and future hope.

A friend of mine once attended a summer school in one of Europe's capital cities. Although the course attracted people of many beliefs and of none, it was led by a fervent evangelical Christian. The professor had many qualities, but subtlety was not one of them. If a lecture, conversation or question provided him with the slightest opportunity to present the gospel, he would jump straight in. On one particular afternoon, the professor was guiding the class on a tour of the local cathedral. As the class wandered around this ancient, frescoed monument, the temptation proved too great for him to resist. 'If you want to know what makes the church beautiful,' the professor cried, 'look up, look up! If you want to know how this world works, look up, look up! If you want to find the only hope, look up, look up!' As the students lifted their heads, they saw the most powerful paintings of the biblical story. By reminding them of how God acted for his people in the exodus, Jesus was asking Cleopas and his companion to look up. When we look to God's story we inevitably see God staring back at us. As with history, in him our past, present and futures begin to make sense.

Although it is crucial in God's big picture, the celebration of the first Passover must rank among the most unusual of all religious feasts. To anyone outside of Moses' camp, and possibly to many within, it must have appeared positively barmy. After plagues, infestations and protestations, Pharaoh belligerently rebuffed Moses' pleas for liberation. God's people had nowhere to go. Given the ruler's intransigence and the desperately low morale of his people, the next phase in God's strategy for liberation must have seemed nothing short of insane. The people were told to organize a freedom feast in every house and home. They were to celebrate their freedom while still in captivity. On that fateful night, or so the promise went, God would rescue his partiers and reward their faithfulness with freedom. By instructing his people to celebrate, Moses was not trying to raise their spirits. This was not an Old Testament rendition of 'Always look on the bright side of life!' God was offering his people the opportunity to do something astonishing. He was asking Israel to forget their present context and commit to his future. By responding to the instruction, God's people stood up to, and escaped, their captors. By releasing a nation, God enacted one of the greatest miracles of all time.

In the exodus, we see an eternal blueprint of what it means to be God's people. This community is no longer stuck in the past or the present. They have decided to live in anticipation of God's future. In this, Cleopas' ancestors teach us what it means to pray and worship, to feast and celebrate. A few years ago a friend of mine died of cancer. What made this experience all the more challenging was that Rob had been miraculously healed of cancer only a few years earlier. Having confounded medical science once before, his faith and hope made it clear that God could do it again. Tragically, it was not to be. As does any difficult and premature death, Rob's death raised many questions. Why would God heal him the first time and not the second? As with many similar questions, the answers are simply beyond us. However, we can say this. Rob's healing was not a miraculous end in itself but rather a hopeful means to an eternal end. The first healing formed the prelude to a second, and far greater, healing of a kind that only occurs in new creation. As for Lazarus, and for any of us for that matter, healing here was not an insurance against death but a promise of a new and eternal life beyond death. His healing was a party in preparation, a celebration in advance, and an anticipation of the eternal freedom that Jesus' resurrection will one day make possible for all.

For Cleopas, the exodus story was a reminder that God's people were a people of promise. With many trials and tribulations ahead, there could be no more relevant training session than this. Cleopas, along with many of Jesus' followers, would in time pay a great price for his faith. And yet he would do this gladly in anticipation of the eternal future which Christ had set before him.

Old story next chapter

In the same way that it helped Cleopas to discover his place in God's story, the exodus also enables us to find where we fit into God's hope for creation. One of the most notable aspects of Luke's narrative is surely Cleopas' failure to recognize Jesus along the way. Jesus' resurrected body was not instantly recognizable to those he appeared to and, with hindsight, Cleopas remarked that it was Jesus' teaching that provided the best clue to his identity. For no one else they'd ever heard could tell God's story like he did. And when Jesus talked about the exodus, Cleopas should have known.

Only hours before his arrest, Jesus shared one last meal with his disciples. The feast of the Passover was drawing near, and Jesus instructed his disciples to make the necessary preparations so that they might celebrate together (Lk. 22:7–38). The disciples followed Jesus' instructions and set the scene. However there appears to be something missing. At no point does Luke mention a lamb, and the lamb is the central ingredient in the Passover meal. How could these faithful Jews have forgotten the lamb? The answer is simple. Jesus' Last Supper occurred just before the official celebration. Luke records the evening as taking place on the Feast of Unleavened Bread. On this day the lambs which Jewish families were to use for their celebrations were slaughtered and prepared at the temple. Like a forgetful cook trying to buy turkey on Christmas Eve, the disciples would have had no chance of purchasing a lamb on this day. But how could Jesus celebrate the Passover without a lamb? After all, it is the lamb that takes away the sins of God's people.

Exactly when the penny dropped we'll never know, but at some point the disciples must have caught on. For as

Jesus began the Passover meal he broke bread and declared: 'This is my body broken for you.' Here, before their very eyes, was the Lamb of God, the one who would take away the sins of the world. There was no need to buy a lamb, for the Lamb of God was seated at the table and about to shed his blood to pay the price of sin and death and purchase life eternal for God's people. On this fateful night and over this sacred meal, Jesus told the exodus story one more time. In the same way that God revealed himself and liberated his people through Moses, he intervened through Jesus. Jesus' Passover was not the last meal of a condemned man but rather a celebration of the miracle to come. As in Egypt, God had not ignored his people's plight. Through Jesus, he would set his people free – once and for all.

In the song 'Peace on Earth', Bono, the lead singer of U2, sings of the difficulty humans have in squaring a belief in God's benevolence with the realities of our broken world. Sometimes, no matter which way we look, 'hope and history won't rhyme'. And yet when we, like Cleopas, open our eyes to the risen Jesus and watch him break bread before us, the world begins to make sense. In this moment we begin to grasp that all our stories fit somehow into God's big story. In Jesus we find one who can make sense of our past, present and future. He has dealt with the sins of the world and secured hope. In him, hope and history do start to rhyme. Wherever we find ourselves on our journey – whether stuck in captivity, wandering in the wilderness or entering the promised land, we can be sure of one thing: The hopes and fears of all the years are met in Christ tonight.

5

Hope Comes
to Dinner

The road ahead

In this chapter we'll look at the church, God's hopeful people here on earth. In Emmaus, Jesus led an inaugural church gathering by breaking bread with Cleopas and his companion. From that point on, God's story would come to life in the community of people who walk, talk and eat with the living Jesus. In the lives of these people, the resurrection becomes more than a rumour.

As we explore the next part of Luke's resurrection story we'll discover another key to hopeful living. By giving his Holy Spirit to the church, Jesus enables his followers to carry out his mission in the world. In the power of the Spirit, the church is free to translate the good news of Jesus into every culture and community, tongue and tradition. By breathing in the Holy Spirit, Cleopas, his companion and disciples everywhere breathe God's life into the world.

Finally, in this chapter we'll explore the implications of these stunning truths for disciples everywhere. God challenges and charges all of Jesus' followers to bring his hope to the world. Cleopas and his companion are the first in an unending line of disciples who will give their lives to tell his story. By joining this community we learn and, in turn, teach the world to live hopefully ever after.

> As they approached the village to which they were going, Jesus acted as if he were going farther. But they urged him strongly, 'Stay with us, for it is nearly evening; the day is almost over.' So he went in to stay with them.
>
> When he was at the table with them, he took bread, gave thanks, broke it and began to give it to them. Then their eyes were opened and they recognized him, and he disappeared

from their sight. They asked each other, 'Were not our hearts burning within us while he talked with us on the road and opened the Scriptures to us?'

They got up and returned at once to Jerusalem. There they found the Eleven and those with them, assembled together and saying, 'It is true! The Lord has risen and has appeared to Simon.' Then the two told what had happened on the way, and how Jesus was recognized by them when he broke the bread (Lk. 24:28–35).

Eyes wide open

Having wandered from Jerusalem to Emmaus in the company of a certain stranger, Cleopas and his companion invited him to dinner. In just seven miles they have journeyed from Christ's crucifixion to creation and back again. Their walk through the Law and the Prophets complete, they sat down to eat. And now, with their eyes wide open, they recognized the risen Jesus. A certain rumour had come true and, with it, something new was just beginning.

Traditionally, Pentecost is celebrated as the birth of the church. However, certain theologians have identified other possible beginnings. Some argue that the church was born at Cornelius' conversion and the subsequent Gentile Pentecost. Others point to the exodus or when Christ was conceived in Mary's womb. In fact, the his-tory of the church comprises many crucial moments and formative events. With that, I'll propose another. Here in Emmaus, in the moment when God's Spirit opened Cleopas' eyes to the Saviour sitting right in front of him, as the risen Christ broke bread and shared fellowship with two of his followers, a new church was born.

While I was at university, a few friends pulled off an amazing stunt. Resisting the usual urge to spend their money on beer, they clubbed together to offer a £5,000 prize to anyone who could make a compelling case against Jesus' resurrection. On the day of the debate, hundreds of students and faculty turned out to hear a local professor take on a Christian apologist. And, although it was almost too close to call, the final decision went the way of the sceptic. So what were my friends to make of the outcome? Should they have packed up and gone home? Could they conclude from this that the resurrection rumours were merely the product of the overactive imaginations of Cleopas and others? To conclude that one discussion can disprove the event is clearly ridiculous. Of course, the same should be said on the other side. I have heard the stories of numerous triumphant apologists in similar debates. And yet, while I am hugely encouraged by and grateful for their efforts, I could not say that any of them is capable of proving the resurrection beyond any doubt.

Recent judicial history demonstrates how hard it is to establish certain proof in a historic event. Although one court found O.J. Simpson not guilty of murder, another blamed him for the death of his wife. Although this was a comparatively recent event that received inordinate media coverage and had highly sophisticated forensic evidence at its disposal, it still proved impossible to make a watertight case one way or another. It is hardly surprising, then, that the outcome of a debate concerning an event that occurred two thousand years ago is less than certain.

While Christian faith, as we will soon see, presupposes the resurrection of Jesus, it does not ask us to become doubt free. The pressure to follow Jesus without a doubt has, for

too long, undermined the journey of many earnest followers. This kind of simplistic faith, which curtails all questions
and denies doubt, simply doesn't work in the real world. If
we could ask Cleopas, I'm sure he'd affirm that it really was
Jesus who broke the bread. And if we asked him if he ever
doubted again, I'm sure he'd have a great giggle at our
expense. We must be careful not to turn the Christian faith
into the Christian facts. None of this is to say that the historical evidence for the resurrection is missing. In fact, given
all of the evidence available, I would suggest that the bodily resurrection of Jesus is the only reasonable explanation
for these events. The story of Christ's resurrection comes
with compelling evidence. I am convinced that the stories of
Jesus' resurrection are more than rumours. However, the
decision to put our lives on the line will forever require an
act of faith and, in turn, this faith will always leave room for
doubt.

In their bid to find certainty, many have mistakenly
attempted to divorce facts from faith. However, any scientist
worth their salt will confess that faith plays a role in the
most factual deduction. Likewise, theologians argue that
faith is a decision based on reasonable facts. After all, no disciple follows Jesus because it doesn't make sense. Whether
we are considering the resurrection story or the force of
gravity, our beliefs comprise a conversation between fact
and faith. In the case of the resurrection, the faith of the
church is the key fact to consider. There is simply no other
reasonable explanation for the church's existence, either
then or now. After Cleopas returned to Jerusalem to share
the news with the others, Jesus' followers sparked the
fastest-growing, longest-lasting and most deeply significant
movement in all history. What's more, they themselves were

transformed from their sorry state of fear, grief and hope-lessness into a society of God-giving, hope-heralding, death-defying individuals. When others demanded an explanation for this transformation, they simply replied, 'He has risen!' In short, through the life of his church the rumours of Jesus' resurrection became certain. This is as true today as ever it was. With rumours of Christ's resurrection still doing the rounds, we needn't look far to find evidence. The willingness of sound-minded Christian students to stake their money and their lives on the living Jesus is just one small example.

In almost no time at all, Cleopas discovered that Jesus had died for us, rose for us, walks, talks and eats with us. He was so confident of this that he walked with Jesus for the rest of his days. How do we follow in his faithful footsteps? We make sacrifices so that others might know that Jesus is alive. We give up hard cash, make difficult life choices, take on seemingly impossible challenges and love without counting the cost. We demonstrate that we can be free from sin, have no fear of death and live only for Jesus Christ our Saviour and Lord. We provide for the hungry, bring healing to the sick and make God's justice flow like rivers. We take time to immerse ourselves, through prayer and study, in God's story. We follow him more nearly and endeavour to become more Christ-like. Put simply, we lead a life for which there can be no explanation other than the presence of the living Christ within us. As others walk and talk with us, we humbly pray that God will open their eyes to see that the rumours are certain, that the risen Christ is real.

Anne Rice became famous for her series of gothic novels, *The Vampire Chronicles*, the most famous of which became a film starring Tom Cruise and entitled *Interview with a*

Vampire. A lapsed Catholic, Rice had always wanted to write about Jesus. She was well known for the historical detail of her work, and she set about the research. Having read much scholarly material, both faithful and sceptical, Rice came to the conclusion that there is only one plausible explanation for the gospel events, the life of the church and, for that matter, Western civilization. None of the above would have been possible, she asserted, had it not been for the death and resurrection of Jesus. Rice sought out her nearest church and attended confession. In the afterword to the novel she wrote as a result of her search, *Christ the Lord out of Egypt*, Rice powerfully outlines her testimony. She admits that the book might irrevocably damage her popularity as an author. After all, finding religion is not what one expects from one of the world's best-selling horror writers. However, Rice knows that faith in Jesus meant putting your whole life on the line. In short, having witnessed the truth of the living Jesus at work in the church and the world, she decided to walk with him and suffer the rumours.

The story of the walk to Emmaus incorporates many mysterious elements. However, one in particular niggles away. Why does Luke only name Cleopas and not his companion? In some stories the gospel writers identify specific individuals (Peter, James, John, Mary, Martha Lazarus and so on) and in others the characters remain anonymous (the demoniac, the rich young ruler and the generous widow, for example). But in this story we have a curious mix of both. There are a number of theories surrounding this mystery, one of which proposes that Luke names Cleopas so that, after Jesus' ascension, those wishing to enquire further about the rumours of Christ's resurrection can search him out. By naming him, Luke singles Cleopas out as one of the primary witnesses for the defence. He was an eyewitness trusted to testify as to the certainty of these rumours. When Jesus opens Cleopas' eyes to the reality of his resurrection, he thereby commissions him to share certain hope in an uncertain world.

Passing the baton

Luke doesn't say whether Cleopas was at the Last Supper. According to Matthew, Jesus shared this meal with the twelve. But whether he'd been there or not, Cleopas would surely have heard the details of this dramatic Passover meal from the others. Cleopas would therefore have understood the significance of Jesus revealing himself through the breaking of bread. Breaking bread like this was both a regular mealtime routine and the hallmark of Jesus' ministry. This simple ritual and prophetic performance defines Jesus' mission. Jesus served Cleopas, in the same way that he has served billions since, by breaking open God's hope in their presence.

I've heard a lot of sermons and read many books. And while it is mainly the stories that stay with me, occasionally a line sticks no matter what. One such phrase is from a book called *The Household of God* by a hero of mine called Lesslie Newbigin. Newbigin's take on the Last Supper is fascinating. He portrays the disciples as confused and scared, as yet unaware of what Jesus is about and unsure of what he will do. And he describes Jesus as a worried Messiah. About to die for a hapless band, he contemplates the possibility that his cause maybe hopeless – not due to his own failings but rather to the ineptitude of those he leaves behind. Judas has already betrayed him. Peter will deny him and, along with James and John, he won't even make it through the next prayer meeting without falling asleep. Can these men really be trusted to carry out Jesus' mission after he has gone? After all, if even those closest to Jesus don't get it, what hope is there? If they are the foundation of the future church, then the gates of hell will most probably prevail. Jesus, in Newbigin's portrayal, is searching for a sign or an act – some form of object lesson by which to ram his mission home. One can almost see him, with furrowed brow, tarrying for a gesture symbolic and shocking enough to capture the corporeal imagination. And then, in a moment, he gets it. Newbigin writes, 'At that moment, when all faith was crumbling, he staked all upon a deed. He took bread and wine, and told them, 'This is my body given for you, this is my blood shed for you. Do this in remembrance of me." '[1]

Newbigin's portrayal is a powerful one. If they only understand and remember this one act, the disciples will have grasped what following Jesus is all about. In the uneasy air of the Last Supper, Jesus breaks bread to help his friends understand his own story. At the table in Emmaus, with the atmosphere about to become one of unimaginable celebration, he repeats the act and commissions Cleopas and his companion as messengers of the resurrection story. As Jesus repeats these inaugural communions on numerous occasions after his resurrection he sets a rhythm for his people. As we share a meal together we remember him and what he did; we remember his take on the big story; we remember how we fit into that story; we remember that he is alive and working in

---

[1] L. Newbigin, *The Household of God* (London: S.C.M., 1953), 67.

us for the hope of creation. In these sacred meals, we remind the world of the eternal hope of the risen Christ. For the communion meal is never simply an internal family affair. It is a proclamation of Christ's death, resurrection, real presence and future coming. As we partake in this meal his story becomes our story and we remember what it means to be his hopeful ambassadors to creation.

My wife has banned me from any kind of do-it-yourself home improvement. I can't say I blame her. In fact, I'm hugely relieved. She has asked that I desist for two reasons. The first is that I'm useless and the second is that the effects of my uselessness make me very grumpy. My first attempts, which also should have been my last, were definitely the worst. We had moved into our first apartment and needed to put up some bookshelves. In hindsight I realize that I bought bad shelves, inadequate screws and not enough of either. Having screwed the shelves into the wall I proceeded to position the books on said shelves. It should be mentioned at this point that I like big books. I placed lots of these hefty, hard-covered tomes upon the shelves and stood back to admire them. After all, what else are books for? After a minute or so of smug, self-satisfied admiration I noticed that the books seemed to be moving closer towards me. Before long, I heard a crash as one of the shelves snapped. With no thought of personal safety, I threw myself against the shelves. My arms and legs were outstretched and every part of my body was slammed up against them in an attempt to push the books onto the shelves and the shelves back into the wall. But, alas, it was not enough. There were simply too many books and not enough me. As, one by one, all twenty-nine volumes of the *Encyclopaedia Britannica* fell on my head, I made a mental note to place these particular books on the bottom – something I promptly forgot due to concussion. Spitting out the volume that had become wedged in my mouth, I screamed for Charlotte to come and save me. When she had finished laughing at the sight of me forcing myself upon our home library, she helped to take the books down and enabled me to loosen my embrace. Now, it goes without saying that, after drilling a whole new set of holes, hanging more supports and restacking the books, exactly the same thing happened again. By the time I finished the job for a third time, about a month or so later, there were so many holes in the wall we would have been better to knock it through. After a decade of such adventures in home improvements, Charlotte instituted the aforementioned ban.

If Newbigin is correct in his unflattering appraisal of the disciples' ability to carry Christ's message, wouldn't Jesus have been better off resorting to Plan B? After all, if God's hopes rely on this motley crew, he's taking a huge risk. Asking the question in front of the mirror, I become doubly concerned. If the hope of Jesus' resurrection relies on someone as dysfunctional as me, what hope is there? I mean, I can barely place a Bible on a shelf without causing the equivalent of a bibliophile's Armageddon. Is God really expecting me to help people find their place in his story? Newbigin's portrayal of the Last Supper is particularly poignant at this point. Jesus' desperate vexations are caused precisely because he knows that there is no Plan B. As we saw in Chapter 3, from the beginning there was only one plan for how God's perfect hope would materialize within creation. This hope rests on his people.

This hope rests on us no matter how inadequate we feel as God's people. No matter how badly we mess up, Jesus persists in his plan to use us. What's more, he trusts us so much that he neither wants nor needs a back-up. We are his story, no matter how much we stutter and stumble. We are his actors, no matter how many cues we miss or lines we mess up. We are his hope, no matter how hopeless we feel.

As someone somewhere once said, 'Never doubt that a small group of highly committed people can change the world. It's the only thing that ever has.' On that night in Emmaus, two people watched Jesus take bread and break it. Over the weeks that followed, as many as five hundred saw him do the same. This small band of highly-committed yet deeply-flawed folk went on to change the world. And it is just as well that they did, for there was no Plan B and we would not be here without them.

Breathing deeply

Having seen the beginning of the next chapter in God's story, Cleopas headed back to Jerusalem. There he updated the rest of Jesus' friends on the latest resurrection sighting. But surely it would take more than Cleopas' story and a few more sightings of Jesus to transform these men and women into the firebrands which Jesus requires. According to Luke, the disciples barely had time to take in Cleopas' news before Jesus appeared to them en masse. Minus the lengthy warm-up that Cleopas was treated to, Jesus' appearance initially struck fear in the hearts of the disciples. However, he proceeded to pronounce peace upon them.

John's account of this incident includes a moment of dialogue and action absent from Luke's account. With his friends believing that he had indeed been resurrected, Jesus said, 'As the Father has sent me, I am sending you.' And with that he breathed on them and said, 'Receive the Holy Spirit' (Jn. 20:21–22). Perhaps this moment when Jesus gave his Spirit there marks the birth of the church. Although Luke omits this particular detail, he records Jesus' promise to send the Spirit soon – which sets up the perfect cliffhanger for the sequel. And, sure enough, Luke's second book, the Acts of the Apostles, begins with a flashback to this promise. Although the details are different, the point that John and Luke are making is the same. If the disciples are to become the story of Jesus' resurrection, they require God's Holy Spirit. For it takes the very breath of God to tell his story adequately.

No doubt all of us can identify someone who has brought God's story to life for us. We've discussed Lesslie Newbigin's powerful portrayal of the Last Supper. It was my great privilege to call Lesslie a friend. Early on in my ministry, thanks to a generous and enterprising friend, I spent many an afternoon reading to Lesslie in the retirement home where he lived. Lesslie was then in his eighties and going blind, so he had recruited an army of readers to keep him on track with his writing and speaking commitments. I have many precious memories of the times we shared – the way he poured the tea, his patient explanation of points I couldn't understand (which at times was most of them) and the uncomfortable wicker chair and the semi-permanent indentations that it made on my backside. But for all our great dialogues and debates, the conversation I remember most was the one I had with myself, every time, as I walked back to the station to catch my train home. 'Was it Lesslie that I was with back there,' I would ask myself, 'or was it Jesus?' The answer to my question was, ever and always, 'Yes.' For whenever I spent time with Lesslie, it seemed as though we were joined by Jesus himself. I can only explain it like this: Lesslie was a man who had inhaled God's Spirit so deeply that he could breathe the very life of Jesus into the stories he told and the fellowship that he shared.

Another friend of mine is a writer and philosopher. We met while studying together in London. I had enrolled on the course because Lesslie told me it would be good for me. Chris had applied because he wanted to work out whether the rumours about Jesus were true. Over the months we spent studying, Chris and I shared numerous discussions. However, for all their lectures and tutorials, these eminent professors couldn't give Chris the certainty he searched for. I was of little use, for Chris was far more intelligent than I am. One day he asked me what had convinced me that the Jesus stuff was more than fanciful rumour. I responded by telling him about Lesslie and the conversations I had with myself. A few weeks later, Chris seemed particularly keen to meet up.

'I've done it, I've found it,' he said. He proceeded to tell me the most remarkable story. A family member had put him in contact with a Greek Orthodox monk who lived as a hermit in a forest in Wales and painted icons. This hermit had hardly withdrawn from the human race, however – hundreds of people visited him every year. He would spend time with each of them, share food and pray for them. Chris had visited the hermit that weekend and finally found the certainty he was looking for. He was so excited, in fact, that he had already booked to go on an Easter pilgrimage with the monk to Mount Athos in Greece.

For all our talk of the evidence for Christ's resurrection, what brings this event home most is seeing Jesus alive in other people. When his story comes to life in our presence, the rumours of his resurrection take on flesh and become more real. But where did Lesslie Newbigin and Chris' hermit find this power? The answer is simple. As Paul writes, they were filled with the Spirit who raised Christ from the dead (Rom. 8:11). While such people breathe air like everybody else, they also draw on God's Spirit, the very essence of God's life and the power of Christ's resurrection. However, an important point of clarification is now necessary – otherwise we will commit heresy and exalt two humans to the position of demigods. It is not simply that Jesus breathes his spirit into a small and saintly chosen few. As Luke reports in his account of Peter's sermon at Pentecost, disciples both young and old, male and female all receive God's Holy Spirit. Having brought about the last days, the power of Jesus' resurrection is available for all people (Acts 2:17–18). For this reason, the New Testament views all believers as God's saints. When we recognize that God's Spirit is within us, it becomes a whole lot easier to live out his story and go about his work.

I have already mentioned my complete lack of expertise as a handyman. But there was one job that I completed with aplomb. Yes, before I was banned from even contemplating home improvements, I tiled our bathroom. And, I'll have you know, I did a most excellent job. I have to admit that I did have some help from a neighbour called Les. While I did in fact put every tile in place with my own impractical hands, Les, a handyman's handyman, stood by, guiding me and instructing me what to do. At the end of the day, not only had I survived the experience but every tile was also still attached to the walls. Les paid me the most incredible compliment. 'I think you now tile as well as me,' he said. In my tiling project, I needed to be shown how to do it. In our Christian lives, we are too often like the novice DIY enthusiast who doesn't bother to read the instructions. We need to avail of the spiritual resources made available to us. Neither Lesslie nor Chris' hermit had reached a special level of enlightenment. What they did do was recognize that God had made Jesus available to them day by day and made it a priority to keep company with the one who walked alongside them. They also knew that Jesus had given them his Holy Spirit and so they learned to breathe deeply. It was as simple as walking and breathing. Having learned to do these things, they told God's story as if Jesus was telling it himself.

I was brought up in The Salvation Army and learned to play a brass instrument when I was very young. In my time, I was a half-decent trombone player. Or at least I was better at the trombone than I am at home improvements. However, one thing held me back from being a really good trombone player. I never learned to breathe deeply. On a daily basis, most human beings only use a small proportion of their lung capacity. To play a brass instrument well requires the performer to access a far greater level of lung power. For a while, I was taught by the principal trombonist of the London Symphony Orchestra. During one lesson, in a moment of apoplectic frustration, Dudley said to me, 'I want you to find a large staircase and run up and down it ten times. After that, when you've collapsed in a heap and are gasping for breath, remember how it feels. That's how you should be breathing every time you blow your trombone!'

The disciples we admire most are the ones who make the risen Christ come alive for us. They do this because they have learned to breathe God's Spirit deeply. They are, rightly, the heroes of our faith – not because they have something which we don't but rather because they have learned to draw deeply on someone who is in us all, namely God's Holy Spirit. In the same way that God's Spirit raised Christ to life from the grave, he longs to raise Christ to life in us. As with the breathing exercises that Dudley put me through, we must learn to exercise the power of the Spirit. Rather than drawing on him in moments when we feel a need or feel especially spiritual, we must learn to breathe his life into every aspect of our lives. We must learn not to give in to silly and petty sins. After all, by Christ's revelation and the power of the Spirit we know that this is not the way to true life. We should not live, as Dallas Willard says, as 'vampire Christians' – disciples who are only after Christ's blood. We must allow the good news of the resurrection to infect every area of our lifestyle, to infuse our time, relationships, community and church with his hope. We should go to the places where Jesus calls us to go, as fast as we can and with as much passion and vigour as we can muster. Then when we find ourselves stretched, challenged and tested, we must remember how it feels because, in this moment, we are breathing God's Spirit deeply.

Friends of mine planted a church in an area of great deprivation. When they had been there for about six months they got talking to some of the young people they had been working with since their arrival. 'Do you ever think about God?' one of the team members asked.

'Funny you should ask that,' was the reply. 'Before you guys came here, we never thought about God at all. But since you arrived, we think about him all the time.' The willingness of these disciples to stretch themselves to their limits meant that others witnessed the resurrected Christ. They not only told God's story; they became God's story. Having breathed deeply of the Holy Spirit, they acted out the resurrection story in their new-found community. As a result, Jesus came to life in and through them and, boy, did they do a great job! Similarly, the life-changing revelation of the resurrection and the infilling of the Holy Spirit enabled Cleopas to tell others about Christ. Within a matter of years, most of civilization would be talking about him. If we can learn the same lessons, then Jesus will surely have the same telling impact on the streets where we live.

The church as God's story

Although Cleopas has only a minor role in Luke's gospel, he went on to become a prominent leader in the early church. This is the second reason why Luke identifies him by name. He is, again, singled out so that others can single him out. Having become a leader in the church at Jerusalem, Cleopas helped to lead the community of Christ's resurrection in this key city. In the years to come, through Cleopas' story, many others would become part of God's story. At a time when the gospel was not available in hard copy, Cleopas translated the story of Jesus for countless enquirers and seekers.

For a short while I had the honour of attending one of Great Britain's ancient universities. I could never get over how many ancient traditions this institution had acquired. This place had traditions from before tradition existed. The memory of my graduation ceremony stands out in particular. Apart from an initial welcome and warning, the entire ninety-minute ceremony was conducted in Latin. This lent the occasion the most enormous sense of decorum and history – until it came to certain subjects, that is. For certain contemporary disciplines do not lend themselves to a dead language. For example, describing the complex and technical details of robotics, cybernetics or gene theory is nigh on impossible if the subject in question was invented several centuries after the language died out. What soon became clear was that some poor doctoral student in the classics department had created new Latin words and phrases to describe these areas of study. The most memorable of these came with the appointment of a new professor of virology who, when his title is translated back into English, became a 'Professor of Noxious Vapours'. I couldn't help wondering whether they had advertised the post under this title and, if so, how many responses they'd had.

As we discovered in the previous chapter, part of the genius of God's hope is that it happens in story form. Regardless of what language we speak or what period we live in, a story is always a story. There may well be aspects of that story that are harder or easier to translate for certain communities or cultures, but the story can still be told wherever and whenever there is somebody to tell it. It also says a great deal that Jesus never wrote the story down. He didn't, in contrast to founders of other religions, write it all out and ask a community to preserve it. Rather, he told and lived God's story in his time and space and then asked his followers to go and do likewise. In fact, by entrusting the future of his story to his followers he made the story open-ended. In their hands, God's story is free for ever more to be told and taught, enacted and lived in every country and community, in every tongue and tradition.

There is also, however, a flip side to this. For if the gospel isn't told or, worse, gets forgotten, God's story goes quiet and his hopes are unheard. If we don't make Jesus' story known in word and deed, then God has less of a look in with our generation. The exciting, open-ended and ultimately fragile nature of God's story is mirrored in the community of story-tellers who own and proclaim it. The church is only ever one generation from extinction. As the cliché goes, God has no grandchildren, only children. Therefore it becomes impossible for the life of the church to skip a generation – a point which the declining Western church would do well to take seriously. This is part of the reason why there are so many sites which we can identify as the birthplace of the church. Bearing in mind, as we've already established, that God's first hope was for a people, we can presumably safely say that God's hope for the church was born before creation. We should also point out that Christians believe in one Church. Consequently, we in the twenty-first century are part of the same Church that Cleopas helped to lead in Jerusalem two thousand years ago. That said, new parts of the church are born in every time and place. As new generations become born again they plant new churches and groups of church members enact God's story in different communities. In this way the church is, in a sense, born all over again. Put simply, the translation of God's story for the world is the church's business.

William Booth, the founder of The Salvation Army, was once asked for his opinion about a controversial new trans-lation of the Bible. The enquirer was trying to stir things up and hoped that Booth would rage against such populist poppycock. Always ready to surprise, Booth replied by sug-gesting that this one new translation was simply not ade-quate. What we need, he proposed, are newer and more popular versions of the Bible. Only when God's story is being told in the life of every Christian on earth, Booth argued, will we have enough translations of Scripture. In one of the hymns Booth penned, he pushed the idea further.

'We need another Pentecost,' he wrote, 'Send the Fire today!'
Booth had no complaint with the first Pentecost. He wasn't
suggesting God could have done better. His dispute, rather,
was with a nineteenth-century church which, to his mind,
had lost sight of the Spirit that raised Christ from the dead;
failed to make the good news of resurrection known; and so
endangered God's hope for the world. Booth's only hope
was that this community be born again.

As we have said all along, there are many formative
moments in the life of such a dynamic movement as God's
church. We need God's Spirit to equip us to live out his story
in each and every generation. I first met Douglas Rushkoff at
a coffee shop at New York University. Rushkoff is a professor
there and a global guru on new media and contemporary culture. Being a fan of his books, I had a long list of questions to
ask him, among them a question about faith. It appeared to me
that Rushkoff wanted to be an atheist but couldn't go all the
way. 'You're right,' he said, 'but I'm Jewish. I'll probably never
get away from the story.' A few years later we met again, this
time at the Jewish World Service, where he was working at the
time. 'I see you haven't got away from the story,' I remarked.
Rushkoff laughed. Since then, far from extricating himself further, Rushkoff has begun to translate the Bible story into a
series of graphic novels entitled *Testament*. Having once tried
to shake off God's story, he has now come to the conclusion
that the most radical thing he could do to subvert the status
quo and change the world is to tell the old story in a new way
for the next generation. His hopeful suggestion to the next
generation is that they begin a revolution against the mind-
numbing, heart-breaking, soul-killing media culture that
seems to have taken over our world. How are they to do it? By
learning and reliving God's story.

After hearing the resurrected Jesus retelling God's story, Cleopas became a leader of the church in Jerusalem. In leading this new resurrection community he made known the living Christ and opened God's story to a new generation.

Our life, his story

Although twice in this chapter we have addressed reasons why Luke may have named Cleopas in the text, we have not yet addressed the identity of his companion. Who is Cleopas' fellow traveller and why does he or she go unnamed? As we've mentioned, some have suggested that Cleopas' companion might have been his wife. While Luke's gospel makes a special feature of the women in Jesus' life, the fact remains that he wrote in a culture where a woman's word rarely counted. Speculation can only take us so far, however, and for the purpose of this next discussion the anonymity of this person is not unhelpful. For while Jesus shows up in the lives of disciples everywhere, the vast majority of these faithful followers will never write, or be mentioned in, a book. Yet none of this stops God's Spirit from making Jesus live in and through them.

In most major European cities you will find a large tomb consecrated to an unknown soldier. Having been given the full pomp and circumstance of state funerals, these anonymous casualties of war were laid to rest under these majestic monuments. But why create such a fuss over somebody that no one could recognize or identify? For their countries, these soldiers are forever a symbol of all those who fought to save lives and preserve freedom. Their elaborate graves stand as a lasting reminder of the many selfless souls who laid down their lives for their brothers and sisters. To my mind, the unidentified disciple in Luke's account fulfils a similar role. The fact that the identity of this person is impossible to verify becomes irrelevant when we consider the power and the poignancy of their anonymity. She, or he, is a symbol of all those men and women who have sought to follow Jesus along life's road. For this reason we can replace every reference to 'the other traveller' or 'Cleopas' companion' with our own name. It seems that, although perhaps unintentionally, Luke has left a space in the story for us.

As those who walk with the living Jesus, we have become part of this story. Having recognized who he is, we live as his eyewitnesses, storytellers and ambassadors of hope. We have witnessed the wonders of his life, death and resurrection and marvel that he has entrusted the next chapter of the story to us. Ours is the challenge to realize God's hope for creation. We need his Spirit to help us accomplish his dreams for the world. In Charles Dickens' *A Christmas Carol*, the ghost of Christmas future prophesies a frightening future for Ebenezer Scrooge. As with most prophecies of impending judgement, the prediction is conditional upon Scrooge's response. In Dickens' happy ending Scrooge heeds the warning and thus averts a fate worse than death. With a hopeful twist, the story provides a helpful exercise for our purposes. Imagine if that same ghost visited you. Once you had gotten over the fright, what hopeful picture would you want him to portray? What would you like him to predict about your future? How and where will you live out God's story? Where will the hope of Jesus' resurrection take hold through you? After you have painted this picture, contemplate one more question. What changes and decisions must you now make in order for your hopes to come true?

God's story lives because we choose to re-enact it, to breathe our lives into telling it. It isn't simply a story that we read or tell. Like the hope it contains, God's story is a *happening*, an event. It happens when we share a meal, remember Jesus, tell his story, breathe his Spirit and make sacrifices for others. Above all, it happens when we make God's hope available in the world. So committed is Christ to these happenings of hope that he promises to be present in them. He's there whenever we gather, break bread, remember him, love one another, feed the poor, visit the captive, house the homeless, welcome the stranger, clothe the naked and obey him in countless other ways. 'I' never do these things. No Christian can – individually, that is. Whenever 'we' do these things, we do them with Jesus, because in this way he is ever present in our life stories. And we'd better believe it, for he's as good as his word.

Bill Hybels is famed for declaring that the local church is the hope of the world. Ever has it been so. Since Cleopas and the disciples first told God's new story to the world, the church has re-enacted God's story for the world and demonstrated his hope for creation. It is the job of the church to demonstrate and teach what it means to live hopefully ever after.

6

Hope in the Future

The road ahead

Here in this final chapter we will look to the road ahead for Cleopas and the other disciples. They returned to Jerusalem to share the good news, where Jesus appeared once more. Jesus ate with them and taught the Scriptures once again and then commissioned the group to be his hopeful witnesses in the world. The time was coming for Jesus to return to the Father and leave his hopeful mission with his followers.

In the early church, faithful followers carried on Jesus' ministry in the simplest and most powerful of ways. By continuing to eat together, the disciples remembered what Jesus had done and communicated his story to the world. However, as they opened their communion wider and welcomed Gentiles to their fellowship, Cleopas and the disciples caused consternation in Jerusalem. Before long, their mission was challenging the powers of Rome and many of their members paid a heavy price for the hope that they had.

As we explore the role of the church in bringing about God's hopes in the future we remember how Cleopas and the disciples demonstrated the coming of God's kingdom in their own time. In the same way we, the church, must point the way to the future. For the church is always and ever the signpost to God's ultimate hopes for creation.

> While they were still talking about this, Jesus himself stood among them and said to them, 'Peace be with you.'
>
> They were startled and frightened, thinking they saw a ghost. He said to them, 'Why are you troubled, and why do doubts rise in your minds? Look at my hands and my feet. It is I myself! Touch me and see; a ghost does not have flesh and bones, as you see I have.'

When he had said this, he showed them his hands and feet. And while they still did not believe it because of joy and amazement, he asked them, 'Do you have anything here to eat?' They gave him a piece of broiled fish, and he took it and ate it in their presence.

He said to them, 'This is what I told you while I was still with you: Everything must be fulfilled that is written about me in the Law of Moses, the Prophets and the Psalms.'

Then he opened their minds so they could understand the Scriptures. He told them, 'This is what is written: The Christ will suffer and rise from the dead on the third day, and repentance and forgiveness of sins will be preached in his name to all nations, beginning at Jerusalem. You are witnesses of these things. I am going to send you what my Father has promised; but stay in the city until you have been clothed with power from on high' (Lk. 24:36–49).

Calling the witness for the defence

Back in Jerusalem, Cleopas and his companion relayed the events of an eventful day. As if to confirm their credibility as witnesses, Jesus reappeared and substantiated their claims in the flesh. Earlier Jesus had expounded Scripture first and then shared food before revealing himself; but on this occasion he was instantly recognizable. To put ghostly fears to rest, he showed his scars and ate broiled fish. Then he unpacked God's story one more time. Turning to the Law and the Prophets again, Jesus told the disciples where they fit into God's story and commissioned them as his ambassadors of hope.

Jesus spent much of this day travelling backwards in time. The discussions of his death, creation and the exodus all focused on events in the past. It seems fitting, then, that nightfall found Cleopas, his companion, the disciples and Jesus all back in Jerusalem. And yet, as we have said all along, the purpose of every one of these discussions was that Cleopas and friends might better understand the present and be more prepared for the future. Although geographically right back where he started, Cleopas had come a long way in just a few hours. Having been stuck in a most unenviable predicament as the disappointed disciple of an executed leader, his decision to get out and walk on was rewarded with infinite interest. A day which began with endless questions about past events ended with Cleopas firmly established in God's plans for the future. As we draw close to the end of this book, one question appears to shout louder than the others: How can we likewise find our part in God's story and our place in his hope?

When someone makes a marked impression upon me, I have a tendency to talk about them – a lot. With that in mind, this is honestly the last time that I'll name-check Lesslie Newbigin – in this book at least. Since he taught me so much, I was obviously keen to learn the tricks of Lesslie's trade. Of course, there were no tricks – just a faithful commitment to walk with Jesus for, as he was fond of saying, 'Ministerial leadership is first and finally discipleship.' However there was one lesson Lesslie taught me, more a tip than a trick, which has enabled me to locate myself in God's story. Whenever he read the Bible, Lesslie told me, he would do three things. First he would look for Jesus, to see where he was revealed in the passage because, as the central character in God's story, Jesus can be found on every page. Jesus speaks through every page. Second, he would look for himself to find where he could be found. By searching the text in tandem with his own heart, it became possible for him to identify characters or situations which resonated with him. In this way, the Bible became his story, too. Third, he would ask how he should walk, talk or act differently as a result of these discoveries. As a result, every Scripture reading was a divine revelation and prophetic event, an opportunity for Lesslie's today to be transformed by God's tomorrow.

After a fish supper in Jerusalem, Jesus retold God's story to the disciples. Once again, God's future plans relied on them grasping the central role which Jesus plays in Scripture and bringing this revelation into their own lives and mission. All that they read in the Law and the Prophets was but a prelude to what they experienced right there and then. As always, the history lesson was future-focused and forward-thinking. Because they were Easter eyewitnesses, the disciples' futures had become irretrievably joined with his. From that point on, the story of Christ's resurrection was theirs to announce, argue and authenticate. In short, as we have seen again and again, God's hope for the future rested on these disciples. Jesus confirmed this when he commissioned them to take God's hope to all peoples: 'You are witnesses of these things,' he declared. Once he dropped this bombshell, the seriousness of the situation increased.

Stuck in a traffic jam from hell a few years back, I lost concentration and rolled – quite gently, I should add – into the car in front of me. I immediately apologized and admitted liability for the accident. However, glimpsing the possibility of a no-win-no-fee-compensation-claim against my insurers, my victim, having shared some colourful thoughts regarding my character and standing, reported me to the police. Though the proceedings were a formality and, as such, a colossal waste of everyone's time, they were also deeply unpleasant. Sitting in a police station, having one's rights read to you and being summarily questioned by a police officer is a horrible experience – even if you have nothing to hide. If nothing else, the experience deterred me from ever straying onto the wrong side of the law.

Christ's serious commission to the disciples is not necessarily new. All of her many prophets would agree that Israel was charged to demonstrate and embody the truth, goodness and beauty of God. And while other nations maintained that there were many deities in heaven, Israel said otherwise. As a result, where the one true God was concerned, Israel's life as a nation constituted the case for the defence. One poignant example of this arises in the prophecy of Isaiah. In Isaiah 42 and 43, Isaiah comforted God's people at a time of great grief and loss. The mourning which framed their predicament, along with the tough love that Isaiah dished out, is one of a number of parallels with the events of Luke 24. Isaiah registered the hopelessness of God's people who had lost Jerusalem and were dragged to a strange land where they were forced to work as servants of a foreign people and their gods. However, the reason they lost hope was not because of the crimes and misdemeanours committed against them, but rather because they had forgotten their place in God's story. God's people had become blind to all the things that God had already done for them. They had become deaf to his word and forgotten his story (Is. 42:18–20).

In his attempt to restore hope to Israel, Isaiah followed the same tactic as Jesus would take on the road to Emmaus. Having already reminded his people of their part in God's creation (Isa. 40), the prophet went on to retell the story of her ancestors' escape from Egypt. He reassured her that, in this story God's story had become intertwined with the life of his people. He reminded Israel of God's faithfulness and the eternal reliability of his promises. To press home the relevance of the story to the predicament in which Israel found herself, Isaiah went so far as to word it in the future tense. God's word is never simply a text or artefact of ancient history. God's word is always a prophecy of things to come, the promise of his hope and his future. If it were a film, the exodus would most likely be a futuristic costume drama. As with all other parts of Scripture, by retelling what God has done in the past we gain a glimpse of how he will act in the future. In this vein, Isaiah had a habit of using the most imaginative scenes and scenarios in his prophecies. After hearing her story retold, Israel was summoned, with all the other nations of the world, to appear before heaven's high court. The case on this day concerned God's claim to be the one true God. The court was already in session, and one of the courtroom officials asked which of the nations would speak up for their regional gods. Silence fell. There was no response. Not a single nation came forward to make their case. So the clerk called for Israel, God's blind and deaf servant – the one who, up until just moments ago, could barely remember her own story. As she stood in the dock she looked to be in a sorry state. She would have been a dubious choice for a witness to a routine road traffic accident. Surely she wasn't up to a case of this magnitude. Suddenly, God himself addressed her directly. 'You are my witnesses,' he declared (Is. 43:10).

Isaiah's prophecies feature frequently in Jesus' ministry. Jesus' sermons, stories and sayings are infused with references to Isaiah. The book of Isaiah proved invaluable to the disciples as they tried to understand who Jesus was. After all, if Jesus was the fulfilment of the Old Testament prophets, then there is much to gain from exploring one of the prophets that he quoted most often. The significance of Isaiah was not lost on the early church. As numerous scholars have noted, this book had an enormous influence on the first Christian communities. Since the gospels had not yet been written down, the earliest congregations used Isaiah to discover where Jesus, their resurrected Saviour and leader, fit into God's story. This knowledge further equipped them to accomplish the mission for which he had commissioned them.

When Jesus commissioned his disciples in Jerusalem to go and tell God's story to the world, he didn't say it quite like that. Rather, he quoted Isaiah 43:10. Although they might have missed the odd reference before, Jesus' audience, a group of faithful Jews who knew their Old Testament, could not have failed to notice the cosmic importance of this moment. When he used these four words, 'You are my witnesses,' Jesus instructed his disciples to establish, before all the nations, that there is one true God, the maker of heaven and earth. This handful of followers, no doubt still in shock over the events just past, were called to the stand as the case for the defence. From here on, they would be the star witnesses in the case to prove the veracity of God's claims and the authenticity of his story.

While taking this in – and no doubt sympathizing with the ordinary folk who received this terrifying assignment – we should remind ourselves of something. Jesus' cosmic commission was not simply for those few who gathered over a fish supper. He repeated these words to those who witnessed his ascension and addresses them to every other follower who has joined him since. As we walk the roads

that God has set before us, our task is no less than to demonstrate and verify the one true, living God. As the first disciples found, conveying this message in a multicultural and
pluralist world can be very challenging. I once worked with
a local council to develop a new town-wide education
system. The area had huge potential but faced serious challenges, the greatest of which was the ethnic mix of its popu-
lation. Two-thirds of the community came from Islamic
backgrounds and the remaining third were, for the most
part, white and working class. Some years before, tension
between the communities had escalated to boiling point.
With a rise in religious fundamentalism on one side and
neo-fascism on the other, sensitivities were high. Knowing
that many towns and cities would face similar challenges
ahead, the national government looked on with a keen interest. Because it is a Christian church and charity, certain government officials initially greeted The Salvation Army's
involvement with some suspicion. After all, having
Christians around would surely only increase the strain.
However, in every meeting and discussion, we stayed on
message: 'As Christians we believe in the God who created
and cares about every single person on this planet. For this
reason, we will demonstrate our faith by serving every
member of this community, whatever their need or creed.'
Because we reiterated this time and again, the government
officials and stakeholders from every part of the community unanimously invited us to work with them. Together
they decided that a truly Christian response was what that
fractious multicultural community needed if it was to hope
for the future.

Contrary to popular opinion, we are not the first generations to live in a multicultural world. Throughout her history,

Israel knew what it was to live in a community filled with other faiths and deities. Likewise, the disciples were thoroughly conversant with the challenges of multiculturalism. They knew, better than any of us, the challenge of proclaiming the one true God in a multi-faith society. And yet Jesus appointed them to fulfil the prophecy of Isaiah, to stand up before the nations and prove the rumour that there is only one God. As Jesus sent Cleopas and the disciples, so he sends us into a multicultural and multiethnic world, with countless deities and spiritualities. Whatever we do, we must remember our story – the one about the one true God who sent his Son to live, die and rise for the whole of creation. We are the witnesses of this event, the carriers of God's truth and the ambassadors of his hope.

24-hour party people

Having been commissioned by Jesus and filled with the Spirit, Cleopas and the disciples boldly went. But how exactly did they take God's hope into their world? The answer, in the first stage at least, appears simple. They carried on living the life that they had led with Jesus. Only now, when there was someone who needed inspiration, challenge and encouragement, or healing, they themselves provided it. And, of course, it goes without saying that they retained the hallmark of Christ's ministry. They continued to break bread in their homes and, whenever they gathered, food played a big part in the proceedings. For this reason, as my old theology professor used to say, the sharing of a meal became the universal common denominator of church life, the constitution of our life together as God's people.

It is often said that if you can find two theologians who agree with one another, one of them is clearly mad. The saying is not without some element of truth. That said, there are some things on which many theologians agree. One of these areas of agreement is the place of hospitality in Jesus' ministry. Now, they may of course all be mad, but, from reading the gospels, I suspect not. Certain scholars, no doubt in a bid to impress us with their scholarliness, use a different word for this same ministry. They call it *commensality* – a posh word for a group gathering to share a meal together. Whichever word we use, the fact remains that sharing food was an essential part of the lives of Jesus' disciples. More than just a bite to eat, these meals provided an opportunity for the church to celebrate and communicate Christ's resurrection hope. For this reason, the sharing of food, in one way or another, continues to shape many aspects of our fellowship today.

At sixteen years of age, I attended a summer music school. I have one particular memory from that week. As I stood queuing for lunch in the self-service canteen, a Salvation Army officer came up to me. He handed me his business card and said, 'Russell, give me a call next week. I'd love for you to come for dinner.' As one who has done a bit of youth work over the years, I can say with some authority that it was one of the most culturally 'irrelevant' ways in which to reach a young person with the gospel. But the facts remain – in the short-term, I was blown away that a senior leader wanted to spend time with a spotty and insecure teenager. In the long-term, I might not be writing this book if it weren't for Major Samuel Edgar, youth worker extraordinaire. Samuel is one of the most hospitable people I know. He grasps the centrality of commensality like few others. He understands the pure and potent combination of food and friendship. He knows it will never go out of fashion. So much so, that every item he buys is individually blessed by St Michael. On a serious note, somewhere during the many meals that Samuel laid on for me, I began to discover what it meant to really follow Jesus. I'd been in church all my life, but it was only when I started sharing food with an older brother that I understood what it meant to be a disciple.

Given the power and importance of food, I am always surprised by the lack of recipe books in the average Christian bookshop. One can usually find a title on any subject in such an outlet. And yet very rarely does one discover a book about food. Sometimes I think we would do well to pull out all the books on evangelism and replace them with cookbooks and restaurant guides. You see, the hundreds of thousands of words which have been published on evangelism have yet to achieve the desired effect. For the most part, throughout the Western world at least, church numbers are declining. And yet in my experience there is one recipe which almost always works when incorporated into the church's missionary plan. Yes, you've guessed it – I'm talking about food. Where would *Christianity Explored* or *Alpha* courses be without food? Sure we all know people who have enjoyed the course content and format but, let's face it, it's the food that keeps them coming back. If you don't believe me, ask any minister who's tried to run the course without the good stuff. Likewise, if you talk to anyone working with young people or students, they'll tell you that you can get away with any programme, no matter how wacky, mad or random, if the offer of pizza is on the table. One of my favourite local churches is run by two friends of mine in downtown Toronto. One of the most diverse groups you'll ever see, this congregation shares a meal after every service. The amount of time and effort that goes into it is enormous and yet, while the meetings are great, it's when the food comes out that you get the sense that church has really started. As with many great churches through history, the magic ingredient of their meetings is the meal.

Every time I come away from Toronto I make the same resolution. I resolve to eat more. By that I don't mean that I plan to put on weight or pig out more regularly. Rather, I resolve to invite more friends over to dinner, especially those I know who are struggling, people who I don't really know yet or friends who don't know Jesus. I resolve to make food a bigger part of my local church life, my discipleship and my evangelism. To my shame, the decision often goes the way of many a New Year's resolution. Back home I find myself too caught up in all the usual meetings and programmes, strategies and activities that church leaders pin their hopes on. And yet, the next time I land up in Toronto God will graciously remind me that I am once again perfecting the ministry of missing the point. For if I really took my discipleship seriously I'd simply commit to eating more. What would happen if our churches took a leaf out of Luke's books? What would happen if we cut back on the meetings and made more of the eating?

As they continued to follow Jesus after his resurrection, Cleopas and the disciples continued to break bread. It wasn't just a first-century fashion thing, a passing phase. It was the best and most simple way to remember what Jesus had done for them and to celebrate and cement their belief that he was present in their here and now. Every time they sat down to eat they worshipped him again and invited their guests to witness his story.

All over to our place

As Jesus commissioned him, Cleopas could have had little idea as to what lay ahead. One particular controversy awaited this future leader in the Jerusalem church, the size and implications of which would have been unimaginable during these heady times of resurrection appearances. Earlier, we said that the decision to continue Jesus' ministry of hospitality was simple – a no-brainer, some might say. However, within a matter of years carrying out this familiar routine became anything but simple. In hindsight, we can see that this was to be expected. After all, although the meal table provides the setting for some of our most intimate and joyous moments, it can also be the backdrop for the most heated of rows.

When a particular set of parents invited their friends over to dinner, they were keen to establish their credentials as good Christian parents. Accordingly, the mother turned to her eldest and asked, 'Johnny, would you please say grace for us?'

Without hesitation, Johnny barked back, 'No!'

His mum, a little embarrassed by her son's rudeness, tried again but received the same response. With her blood pressure rising, she tried one last time. 'Johnny,' she said, her tight smile barely covering her gritted teeth, 'Just close your eyes and say what your father said at breakfast.'

Every eye was now fixed on Johnny. 'Oh God,' he paused. 'We've got those 'orful people coming to dinner tonight.'

Sharing a meal in Jesus' time was not quite as simple or uncomplicated as it might seem. In fact, dinner dates could easily be the subject of scandal and offence. As in most societies, mealtimes in first-century Palestine came with a strict set of etiquette. The most stringent of the many do's and don'ts had to do with whom one chose to eat. After all, it would not be right to do dinner with "orful people'. Jesus and his disciples were well aware of these rules and customs and so in most, if not every, case their mealtimes were purely Jewish affairs. According to the Law, the act of sharing a meal was about as intimate an interaction as humanly possible, barring sleeping with someone. In this intimacy lay the true power of Jesus' own brand of table fellowship. By sharing food, Jesus welcomed his followers into the future that God had for them – not a future marked by qualified distance or disinterested judgement, but a future awash with closeness, acceptance and intimacy. Despite the fact that he restricted his expression of table fellowship in deference to the Law, Jesus' mealtime practices were still not every religious person's cup of tea. For while he did eat with fellow Hebrews, some of his critics deemed that the moral standing of certain of his dinner guests (Jewish tax collectors and prostitutes, for example) breached the sophisticated etiquette of Jewish law. However, Jesus' response was emphatic. He hadn't come to heal the healthy or feed the fat. He was here to patch up the poorly and fill the famished.

In following his lead, Jesus' followers went one step further and entertained in an area where Jesus did not tread. Inspired by the Spirit, they pushed the hospitality boat right out. They had always included Jews of lesser standing in their table fellowship, but then they began to invite Gentiles to dinner as well. In a context where Jews daily thanked God that they were neither foreigners nor dogs, one can see how this development might cause controversy. However, Jesus' disciples took their call seriously. When he used the words of Isaiah, Jesus had clearly commissioned Cleopas and friends to tell their story to all the nations. If the best way to share this story was through a meal, then it made sense to invite those outside of Israel to join the party. Believing that they had been called as witnesses not just to their countrymen but to the world and his dog, the disciples began to hand out 'access-all-areas' passes to anyone who would join them. But how did they dare to make such a dangerous move?

It all began with the Holy Spirit instructing Peter to welcome Cornelius, a God-fearing Roman centurion, to the party. In hindsight, there might have been more acceptable Gentile groupings to reach out to, however the Sprit was insistent that their first extra-Judaeo invite should be to one of the hated pagan oppressors. By obeying God, Peter kicked off what would become the Gentile Pentecost (Acts 10 – 15). As a result of Cornelius' conversion and baptism and a consequent council of church leaders in Jerusalem, many Gentiles were added to their number. The Jews in Jerusalem were scandalized by the decision to invite these 'dogs' in from the cold and so excommunicated the fraternizers from their synagogues. However, this would not stop Jesus' followers from sharing their hope with the world, and so they continued to meet in their homes, sharing food and worshipping Jesus. One can see why some have pointed to this moment as the birth of the church. From this point on, a once small Jewish sect went global. As we discovered earlier, somewhat like the Queen of England the church has numerous birthdays – and they're all worth celebrating. In this case we celebrate because of the disciples' courageous obedience and determination in offering God's story as the hope of the whole world.

When we watch great dramas we witness twists and turns that we would previously have thought impossible, only to realize with hindsight that it couldn't have turned out any other way. The welcome the disciples extended to the Gentiles in Acts is one such drama. The choice to include them in the church's fellowship was both surprising and predictable. On the one hand, Cleopas never expected to lead a community which would tear down such ancient and sacred rules and regulations. On the other, having heard Jesus commission them as witnesses to the nations and having witnessed the work of the Spirit in Cornelius' conversion, the story seemed destined for this happy and hopeful ending.

As we discussed, Cleopas would have known Isaiah well. He would have known by heart the passages in which all the nations of the world run to join God's banquet in Jerusalem. He knew that the prophet had called Israel to become a 'light to the Gentiles'. What's more, like anyone who's been to a Christian carol service or heard the *Messiah*, he knew that Jesus believed himself to be the fulfilment of these prophecies. Now, while hindsight is a wonderful thing, one can see how the inclusion of the Gentiles in God's story became the logical next step in the fulfilment of God's hope for the world. Having watched Jesus share communion with the fringe members of Israel's family and subsequently heard him call them to be his witnesses to all nations, the disciples invited the world to join the party.

A cursory glance at church history shows the huge advances God's people made as they followed Jesus into the future. In every generation, this remarkable community discovered new truths, reached new lands, toppled despots, changed communities and generally brought God's future closer to our present. However, while God's people have come a long way in two thousand years, the birth of the church remains challenging and prophetic. A few years ago I was teaching on the early church at a conference. During the question time one woman asked, 'My best friend at work is gay. My husband and I want to know whether it's okay to invite him over for dinner and, if so, if he should bring his partner?' At the time, there was a huge rumpus in the church and press about the ordination of practising homosexuals as church ministers. As a result, and somewhat unusually, everyone appeared to be hanging on my answer. To my shame, I stuttered for a bit while I searched for the answer that would upset the least number of people. Catching myself mid cop-out, and feeling suitably appalled by my gutlessness, I relayed the story of the Gentile Pentecost and wished the lady well for her upcoming dinner party.

Most of the readers of this book, like the writer, are Gentile Christians. We have no blood ties to the Israelites but have become God's people through seeing courageous followers, such as Cleopas, paying the price of his faith. By stopping the world from coming to dinner and thereby depriving them of sharing fellowship and experiencing the radical acceptance that was the hallmark of Jesus' ministry and the early church, we not only deny the hope of the world but blaspheme our own salvation. No doubt some will be offended by this and throw lines such as 'Go and sin no more' in my general direction. However, as with my answer to the woman in the seminar, this book is not a disputation on sexual ethics. It is rather an attempt to chart God's hope for the world. The fact remains that a movement which was birthed in the radical inclusion of outsiders has too easily and too often become an institution famed for its exclusivity.

At a time when the world can seem too multicultural to bear, God's people must stick to script and invite the world to dinner. The church was born out of scandalous and subversive acts of hospitality. It was this willingness to break with the past and assert God's future that gave the world new hope. As we share our table we share God's story.

Eat as much as you like

By extending Jesus' ministry of hospitality to all, Cleopas and the disciples invited the world to join the church. The 'people of God', a once highly exclusive society for those with the right family connections, now had an open membership policy which was free to all. However, this is not the only consequence of the Gentile Pentecost. With the admission of other nations, the disciples opened the world to God's future. In the same way that the disciples saw the future of creation in the resurrected Jesus, the world could now glimpse God's future kingdom in the life of his people. In short, the kingdom had come in the person of Jesus and was coming closer through his church.

Sitting with friends in a local restaurant, I had a pang of conscience. Remembering that all meals are sacred occasions and wanting to appear suitably holy, I offered to lead us in prayer. As I drew my short but theologically profound intercession to a close, I opened my eyes to see that a strange figure had joined us. There in front of me stood a man with blonde hair and blue eyes. He was dressed all in white from head to toe and was shining like the sun. With eyes closed he stood, motionless, amongst us. At this point we had all opened our eyes to see him. Our confused expressions hid a corporeal question. Could this really be him? Was it true that the Lord of Hosts had joined us for this special meal? Might it be that he had chosen this restaurant and our company for the first appearance of his second coming? And all this as part of the £12.95 eat-as-much-as-you-like-pre-theatre menu? Around then, we noticed that our Lord appeared to be carrying two objects. But what could they be? One looked like a sceptre, the other like an orb. After a moment longer, and with great calm and poise, he opened his eyes and then did gaze upon us. 'Oh!' he said, 'I forgot where I was for a minute. Do you want any salt or pepper?' Apparently he was a waiter and, having arrived with the condiments during our prayer, had closed his eyes in respect only to get caught up in the moment. I can't blame him – after all, it was a truly heavenly prayer.

As we mentioned in the first chapter, many associate the coming of God's kingdom with a series of large and mystical events. However, joining the church does not launch us into a new heavenly reality far from the things of this world. Life in the church is not akin to being beamed up into the heavenly realms in order that we might spend time with Jesus. The movement happens the other way round. As in his incarnation, Jesus makes himself present on the ground through the church. It is for this reason that we call the church his body. Because of his resurrection, those who follow him today continue the ministry that Christ started in his lifetime. Becoming part of the church means that we increase our commitment to the world by learning to live in hope. If we can crack this, we will provide the world with a new way of living.

The meals that Cleopas and the others shared in Jerusalem were not just friendly get-togethers – they were prophetic demonstrations. Not only did these events offend God-fearing Jews, but they also challenged the universal political power of their day. Not only did they upset the leaders of the synagogues, Cleopas and his friends also threw down a gauntlet for Caesar, the king of the world at the time. In the Roman Empire there was only one legal religion. It was compulsory, therefore, for all to worship the gods of Rome and proclaim Caesar as their earthly personification, both saviour and lord. The only exception to this rule were those troublesome Hebrews. Having been unable to stamp out this particular faith, the Romans agreed to turn a blind eye. Prior to the Gentile Pentecost, the church posed little threat to Rome. For after all Cleopas, like the other believers, was a Jew and thus protected under this exemption. With Cornelius' conversion, however, new issues arose as the movement first welcomed more and more Gentiles and, second, established itself in other parts of the empire. Once again, food was part of the problem. In the meals that they shared together these new disciples remembered Jesus, the one whom even imperial Rome could not put down, and hailed him as their Lord and Saviour. Through his death and resurrection, Cleopas believed that God had crowned and anointed Jesus as the true King of the World. By asserting Jesus' power the church denied the legitimacy of Caesar and, hence, every meal which they shared was a direct challenge against the gods of Rome. In the early church, every member was an active political dissident. A cursory glance through the rest of the New Testament illustrates where this would lead. By the time that John added his final 'amen' to the book of Revelation, countless Christians had walked the way of Christ to execution.

Although our church context may appear less dangerous, the message we send out by our membership is no less subversive than that of our predecessors. The essential truth remains that every gathering of the church and every act of communion is a meeting of dissidents. The church comes together to confront the powers that be, to proclaim to the world that the people who are running the show are not the ultimate power-brokers. We stand together and declare that the world belongs to God and that his hope will out. More than that, we ask that his kingdom might come right here and now, and through us. We invite him to mess up the status quo and let loose his new creation. In this way, every church meeting is a revolutionary statement. We point to the life of the church to show the world what new creation will look like. For the new heaven and the new earth will be a perfected version of the church's present life. As some have suggested, the church stands at the gate of heaven. This doesn't mean that the church gets to decide the entrance exam, but it does mean that we should provide a glimpse of God's hopes for the future.

My in-laws tell a wonderful story about friends of theirs who moved to a new town. Their previous home had been subjected to a steady stream of major building projects. Loft extensions, swimming pools, outhouses, conservatories, garages, patios – you name it and they'd started it but failed to complete it. They had a grand vision for their property yet never quite realized the dream. As a result, they lived on a perpetual building site. My in-laws were going to visit these friends in their new house but knew only the name of the road of their new address. My mother-in-law was concerned that they might not find them. 'Don't worry about that,' my father-in-law replied. 'We'll just drive down the road until we find a house that's only half-built.' And that's exactly what they did. Sure enough, halfway down the road was a substantial property which looked to have great potential but was in the middle of major renovations.

The community of the church straddles two separate worlds. Because we live here, in this fallen reality, our congregations resemble the same broken creation that we see in the rest of the world. By the power of the resurrection, however, we also live in the future, the kingdom of God, where Jesus rules supreme and offers his hope. The balance between these worlds inevitably differs from church to church and from week to week. Some have given up on hope and so believe that the church is just another club or society after all. Their churches are homely, comfortable and unambitious. Others are like the friends of my in-laws. They have a huge vision for how the world could be transformed but never quite get round to the project. In truth, most struggle between the two. They have a vision for how God would have them change the world and they work hard to enact it. Living with this tension is never easy, and often it is painful. However, through it all something remarkable happens.

When we recognize before God that this world is not yet the one that he hopes for, we invite hope to take hold. And by further pledging our allegiance to Jesus, and seeking to go about his business, we contribute the new build, which is his kingdom. In short, by directing others to the way things will be when Christ's rule takes hold of all creation, we enable God's perfect future to infuse our imperfect present with hope for the future. Of course, we don't do this on our own. We are rightly reliant upon the vision of Christ and the power of God's Spirit. Or, should we say, essentially they make the difference. The Spirit raised Christ from the dead and the Spirit makes the church. The Spirit transforms us from being just another club into Christ's body. Jesus and the Spirit are the two key protagonists of the church, be it local or universal. Through them, the church is more than a historical society. We don't get together to explore the work of dead poets or political leaders. We come together to remember Jesus, the one who lived and died and rose again, and whenever we tell his story the Holy Spirit makes Jesus present among us. For this reason, Christ is ever there to help and heal, to guide and direct and to save and surprise. In this we can take great hope, for we do not work in vain but in anticipation of a brand new world.

In no small part, the fall of communism in Romania was due to the faithful witness and dissenting fellowship of the Christian church. On the fateful night when this ex-Eastern Bloc country was changed forever, a crowd of thousands gathered in the capital's largest square. At first they uttered their calls for change with some fear and trembling. For, some hours earlier, one of the country's most high-profile church leaders had been killed by government troops. Amidst great confusion and concern somebody scribbled a note on a small scrap of paper. Before long, the note was being passed around the assembly with growing excitement. This one simple couplet transformed the gathered community. No longer fearing for their lives, they found the confidence to change their world forever. The note read like this, 'If not now, then when? If not us, then who?' When it comes to announcing, proclaiming and providing God's hope for the world, the church must surely ask the same question. If we, the people of God who are filled by his Spirit and joined by the living Christ cannot transform the world, then what hope is there? And in God's church that is only ever a generation away from extinction, if not now, when? However, if we can breathe God's Spirit and live Christ's story, the whole world will discover that they too can live hopefully ever after.

Having undergone the most remarkable commissioning ceremony, Cleopas took hope and hurried towards God's kingdom. Cleopas and the disciples knew that there was no one else to take the news of Christ's resurrection to the world. They were the church, and the hope of the world rested on their shoulders. From this point forward Cleopas' life would be defined by the quest to bring God's perfect hope through an imperfect church. In this, he would both protest against the state of things and demonstrate God's plan for new creation

Come again

After they witnessed the resurrection and were commissioned by Jesus, it fell to Cleopas and friends to seize the moment, to demonstrate the power of God's kingship and the radically different nature of his kingdom. In doing this, they provided a foretaste of what was to come. Their gatherings, while still imperfect, provide us with a glimpse of how the world will be when Christ is all in all. Their fellowship was a window upon new creation as those who came into contact with them miraculously experienced the presence of the risen Jesus.

The atmosphere in the room was tense. The deliberations of this august gathering had stalled at a critical point. It was unsurprising that a decision of such magnitude should vex so. After all, imagine the missional implications and the consequences for the church community, not to mention the effects of such a commitment upon global poverty and world peace. After another prolonged and awkward silence, the minister suggested that the church council take a vote on whether to go for a burgundy Axminster carpet with wool twist or the dark red Wilton with velvet yarn. Jim, the most vociferous member of the council, immediately raised his hand for the Axminster. Nine other members of the council did likewise, mainly because they were scared of Jim. Having asked for a show of hands for the dark red Wilton carpet with velvet yarn, the minister raised his arm more in hope than expectation. His was the only vote. Suddenly, the ground began to shake along with the ceiling. The room filled with smoke, choirs of angels could be heard singing in the background, the vaulted roof cracked open and the auditorium was filled with light. Then, through the smoke, the council could make out a figure. Jesus himself was entering the room. 'Thus sayeth the Lord,' he began. 'I want dark red Wilton with velvet yarn.' That said, he ascended through the gap in the ceiling, the smoke cleared and the angels departed. A solemn hush fell upon the room. Who would break the silence?

'Well,' said Jim, 'it's all very well 'n that but it's still ten votes to two. Burgundy Axminster it is, then!'

When it comes to his presence in the church, we often find it easier to tell Jesus what he should do rather than listen to what he wants to say. While the early church believed that the kingdom was already present, their prophetic expectations were by no means already met. These believers hoped for the day when Christ would return and establish his kingdom rule in full. What's more, the majority believed that this would occur in their own lifetimes. With their belief that Jesus would return quickly, some grew concerned at the delay. Surely, they thought, given the persecution that some of their brothers and sisters were enduring, he'd intervene soon. After all, if Jesus is alive what was there to stop him from coming back forthwith? Having believed that his resurrection had brought an end to death, the loss of family and friends tested the faith of these new believers. They had expected to experience the fullness of his kingdom in their lifetimes.

Although the delay in Christ's return has stretched for almost two thousand years now, we still find ourselves speculating as to the details of his return. The church is home to a perpetual fascination in this regard. In the last few centuries there have been endless theories, studies, films, novels and prophecies about when we can expect the final end times. A friend of mine is fond of saying that, when he was first a Christian, he knew everything. 'I even knew when the world would end. I bought an End of the World Wall Planner from the bearded lady at my Christian bookshop.' As did believers in the early church, Christians today find that their theology grows with them. This means that things we were certain about sometimes become more mysterious and, more importantly, our overly simplistic views develop into deeper and more robust beliefs. However, whether we live in the first century or the third millennium, one thing remains the same. Jesus was remarkably coy about the time, place and nature of his return. In fact, he explicitly states that he doesn't know the hour. While it is possible to compute all kinds of scenarios from the various apocalyptic prophecies within the big story, the fact remains that our hypotheses have always fallen, and always will fall, woefully short when it comes to second-guessing the second coming. I remember prophesying the imminent end of the world to a teacher at school. The sky had gone very dark and it was only three in the afternoon. 'It could be the end of the world, Sir!' I said. Apparently, I was wrong. I don't mention this to be flippant but just to point out that many Christians have poured huge amounts of time, resources and research into prophecies no more accurate than mine. Incredibly, while Jesus has said he himself doesn't know, we remain convinced that we can go one better.

As our journey draws to a close, I want to reinforce what I see as the critical challenge for churches seeking God's hope. Put simply, why hang around waiting for hope when hope is already waiting for us? I was reminded of a cartoon of a policeman and an apocalyptically cheerful street evangelist. The miserable messenger of good news was wearing a sandwich board announcing that tomorrow would mark the end of the world. The policeman looked at him and said, 'If I see you tomorrow, I'm going to nick you under the Trade Descriptions Act.' How many churches do we know that would be vulnerable to such a charge? And yet, all the hope we could ever want is waiting for us in the friend by whose side we walk. All the optimism, vision, imagination, courage and strength we could ever need is right here in the one who breaks bread at our table. As Cleopas found out on the way to and from Emmaus, every miracle we could ever want has already been given to us over a long weekend in Jerusalem. And as Cleopas discovered later, Jesus' miraculous presence remains with his followers forever more.

The church, whether under Cleopas in Jerusalem or our local minister, is the community in which Christ chooses to live. Furthermore any place, person or community where Christ is present as Lord and Saviour is automatically a new creation. As a result, those who wish to glimpse the new heaven and the new earth should take a look at the church. The other day, I was walking back from lunch break with a friend. We were discussing the fact that our church had decided not to have a midnight service on Christmas Eve. I was most disappointed as this is one of my favourite services of the year.

While discussing the alternatives I said, with what turned out to be some volume, 'I really want to do midnight mass but I just don't know where to go!'

At this point the homeless guy who we happened to be walking past shouted at me. 'You wanna' try a church mate?'

Taken aback, I smiled, thanked him for the suggestion and promised him that I would take his advice.

The ending of the story of the Emmaus road is too spectacular to describe. However, in the moments we have left I will try. Having located himself in the very climax of God's story, Cleopas got it. He understood where he had come from and where he was going. He knew how history began, why it had changed and where it would end. What's more, he knew that Jesus – the one who made the world, makes history and perfects all things – was his friend and companion. He subsequently followed his lead and unlocked God's plans for creation. The rest of his story can be summed up in one simple lesson: If we want to live hopefully ever after, we'd better get to church and find Jesus. Because Cleopas and others followed this call, we are here, two thousand years later, walking that road all over again. And now it is our turn to contemplate what might happen if we, like Cleopas, take Jesus at his word.

An actor friend of mine recently found himself on tour in one of the world's major cities. His play, which had won every award going, was the talk of the town. He was being wined and dined by movie stars and producers and life couldn't have been better – or so you would think. One Sunday, he left the theatre where he was working and began walking towards another. In his hand was a ticket given to him by a world-famous actor who had invited him to come and see his play. As he looked down at the ticket, he hit rock-bottom. Lonely, tired and feeling utterly hopeless, he walked into a large church building. Not being a regular churchgoer, he sat at the back and watched the service.

As the preacher went up to speak, he pointed to a large red light above the pulpit. 'In a minute, that red light will come on,' he began, 'and, per every week, the first five minutes of my sermon will be broadcast on network radio stations across the nation.' The preacher paused. 'Only this week, when the light comes on I'm not going to say a word. You see, as I was preparing my word, I sensed the Lord say that there will be thousands of people listening today who are lonely, tired and helpless. These folk have hit rock-bottom and they have nowhere to go. So when the red light comes on, rather than have me preach at them, I want you all to stand and pray out loud together so, if nothing else, they know that we, God's people, are praying that Jesus' hope would come into their lives.'

When the red light came on, 1,500 people simultaneously stood and cried out to God for all those who had run out of hope. And my friend sat at the back with tears pouring down his cheeks.

If any story I know demonstrates the power of the church to bring hope to the hopeless, it's this one. On that fateful Sunday afternoon, my friend walked off the street and into the church. And what did he find? He found hope. He never did make it to the play, which goes to prove another point. Why would you go anywhere else when you can be part of God's story? The Catholic theologian Teilhard de Chardin famously wrote that 'The future belongs to those who can give the next generation reason for hope.' By far his most famous quote, the line has become a bumper sticker, and why not? It is certainly a quote that travels well. Two thousand years ago, Cleopas set out on the road to Emmaus. Having met the risen Jesus, he continued to walk the walk and helped to give God's gracious hope and perfect future to the world. The question for us now is this: Will we do likewise? Will we take our part in God's hopeful story? Will we give hope to the next generation? Will our lives make certain the rumours of Jesus' resurrection? Will we teach our world to live hopefully ever after?